ROAMING MIDSOMER

WALKING AND EATING IN THE MURDEROUS HEART OF ENGLAND

CHRIS BEHAN & MARTIN ANDREW

First published 2016

The History Press
The Mill, Brimscombe Port
Stroud, Gloucestershire, GL5 2QG
www.thehistorypress.co.uk

British Library Cataloguing in Publication Data.
A catalogue record for this book is available from the British Library.

ISBN 978 0 7509 5587 4

Typesetting and origination by The History Press
Printed in Malta by Melita Press

CONTENTS

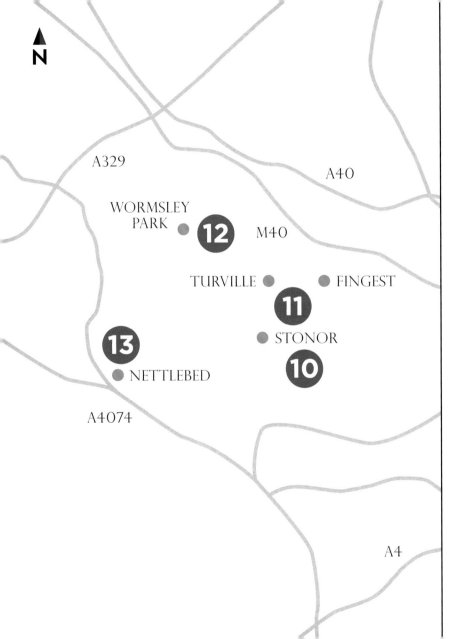

Walk Locations

A329

A40

WORMSLEY
PARK 12 M40

TURVILLE FINGEST
11
STONOR
13 10
NETTLEBED

A4074

A4

CHAPTERS:

● White Ducks and Witchert Walls

● The Ridgeway National Trail

● Red Kites and *The Vicar of Dibley*

● Poohsticks, Clumps and an Abbey

● Preservation Railway Lines

X Walk Numbers

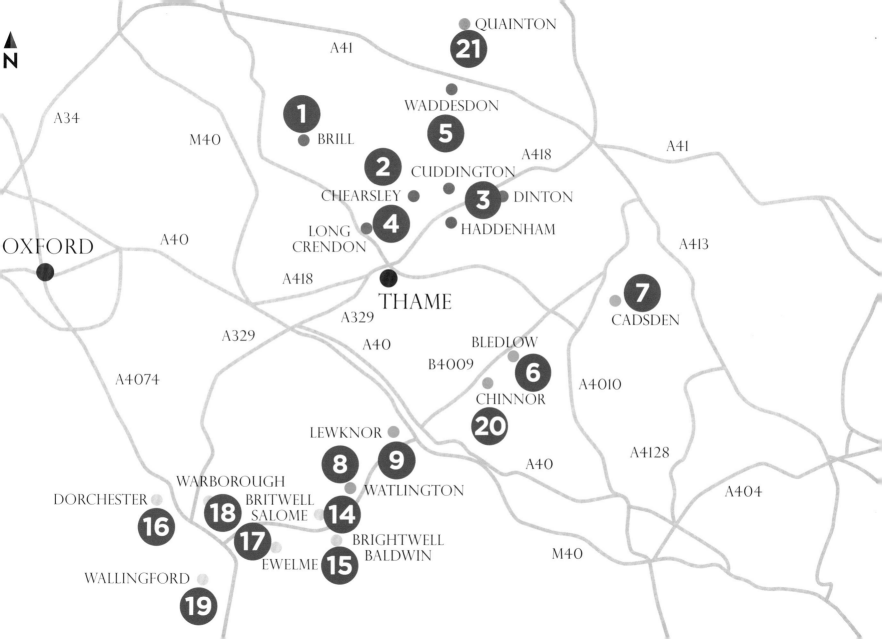

ACKNOWLEDGEMENTS

First, a big thank you to the thousands of people from around the world who have bought *Exploring Midsomer* and to the organisations, from libraries and gardening clubs to WIs and U3As, who have invited me to speak to them about the book. Let us not forget to thank the bookshops, especially the independent ones, who have stocked and sold the book. Without your support, reviews and suggestions, *Roaming Midsomer* would never have been dreamt of, commissioned, written and photographed, let alone published.

All the media organisations that have either interviewed me or reviewed *Exploring Midsomer* deserve a thank you, but special mention has to go to ITV Meridian News for producing a feature item about *Exploring Midsomer* that included the two Inspector Barnabys and myself. Say no more!

Thank you to South Oxfordshire District Council, Sarah Osborne and their visitmidsomer.com website for their tremendous efforts to promote Midsomer tourism in South Oxfordshire and involve me in them.

Midsomer Murders is loved the world over, especially on the Continent. So I have a Eurovision thank you.

The French love *Inspecteur Barnaby* (Sunday evenings on TV France 3), so special thanks must go to the French magazine *BBBmidi*, which wrote a superb review of *Exploring Midsomer*, including a recommendation that the book would make an excellent 'cadeau de Noël'. They even had an 'Inspecteur Barnaby' French competition. The prize? A signed copy of *Exploring Midsomer*.

Martin and I would also like to acknowledge the numerous people we have chatted with on our travels, walking the routes in this book, by field gates, in cafes, pubs and in village streets and fields. We are inveterate 'chatterers' and it makes the walks infinitely more enjoyable and rewarding, if somewhat slower in time terms, but what's the hurry? Enjoy the countryside, villages and towns of Midsomer country on your own terms.

A huge thanks to my book partner in crime, Martin Andrew. I can always rely on Martin pointing me in the right direction on the walks, as well as telling me the history and the significant architectural features of every listed building we pass in Buckinghamshire and Oxfordshire.

Thanks go to The History Press, especially Nicola Guy my Commissioning Editor, for giving me the opportunity to publish not only one book, but two.

To our families and everyone else who has encouraged us and inspired us, yet another thank you.

Finally, the biggest thanks go to Margaret, my wife, and Jill, Martin's wife. Margaret who has suffered me vanishing into the study to tap away on my Apple Mac for hours, days, weeks and months on end, whilst Jill has been an endless source of ideas.

Chris Behan

FOREWORD

After the publication of *Exploring Midsomer* I was asked to talk to the Seer Green and Jordans Book Club, which meets, once a month, at the Jolly Cricketers, Seer Green. At the end of the evening I was chatting to the members and a couple told me that they would use the book as a guide for Sunday afternoon trips around the area. I was really pleased, as this idea had been one of my objectives for the book. Furthermore, it raised a question in my mind. I was encouraging people to visit these English towns and villages but did not suggest anything they could do once there. At this point an idea occurred to me. How about a walk, view the beautiful English countryside and stop at a restaurant, a pub or even a coffee bar. Midsomer towns and villages, like the rest of the world, now have a variety of coffee bars and, I am happy to say, local people run many of them.

So *Roaming Midsomer* was conceived and off I trotted with my idea to chat with Martin Andrew about it. Martin, a friend for nearly thirty years, has written over sixty books and a myriad of articles for the national press, many of them on English history and walking. His knowledge of the English countryside, its history and its listed buildings made him the ideal companion for this adventure.

I will now let Martin carry on the story.

Chris Behan, 2016

INTRODUCTION

Chris Behan's *Exploring Midsomer* was first published in 2012 and has proved something of a best-seller in its field. I greatly admired the book and wrote a foreword for it. It occurred to us when chatting one day that we should take the *Midsomer Murders* theme further and combine Chris's photographic skills and my experience as an 'outdoor writer'.

We both love walking, although with Chris it's a stop-start process as he will take hundreds of photographs on a 5-mile walk. We discussed the idea of producing a book of walks in Midsomer and set ourselves certain limits. We decided that each walk should be around 4 miles, although they naturally vary in distance, and that there should be a good pub, tearoom or cafe either en route or at the end of a walk. This is not a 'walks from pubs to pub' book, although the majority of watering holes are of necessity pubs. Some, such as The Leathern Bottle in Lewknor, welcome dogs and others have beer gardens where dogs are allowed. Most will bring out a bowl of water for your dog if asked.

Catering sorted, we wanted to make every walk a circular one, which means a single family or group of friends can avoid shuttling cars from start to finish and wasting good walking time. The distance is designed to allow a pleasant half-day stroll with the warm promise of refreshment and a bite during or after the walk.

That's the easy bit: the secret of these walks is their focus on *Midsomer Murders* locations. In this volume there are twenty-one routes, all within Buckinghamshire and Oxfordshire, the undoubted heart of *Midsomer Murders* country, although one Buckinghamshire location doubles up as a French location. The walks offer a range of scenery and difficulty. Generally speaking the hillier ones are set in the Chiltern Hills, that wonderful designated Area of Outstanding Natural Beauty. The lowland ones in the Oxfordshire vales and plains and the Vale of Aylesbury are,

in the main, easier going. The Dorchester walk involves ascending the Wittenham Clumps, Brill's name rhymes with hill for good reason (see *Exploring Midsomer* for an explanation of the village's name) and Waddesdon Manor is also on a hill.

Each walk includes *Midsomer Murders* locations, some with a considerable number, and the '*Midsomer* comes to …' section discusses these to varying levels of detail.

A broad assessment of dog friendliness is also included for each walk.

Chris's sketch maps show the routes with most of the stiles, kissing gates and hand gates indicated. However, we strongly recommend carrying an Ordnance Survey map with you, as these sketch maps are indicative and need supplementing, as always in walking books. OS maps at a scale of 1:25,000 show field boundaries and a high level of information, which greatly assists navigation. All the walks are contained on four OS sheets – 170, 171, 180 and 181 – with a small excursion on to sheet 192 for the village of Quainton in Walk 24.

Generally speaking, navigating from the Landranger OS maps at 1:50,000 is not nearly so straightforward: it is surprising how having no field boundaries marked makes lowland walking to such a map unnecessarily difficult and we want to avoid the use of compasses for these walks. If you follow our directions you should have few navigational problems, but bear in mind that stiles are slowly being replaced by kissing gates all over the country to make the countryside more accessible for all.

We were delighted when The History Press enthusiastically supported our proposal and this book, uniform in shape and size with *Exploring Midsomer*, is the outcome. We think it is an excellent sequel to *Exploring Midsomer* and hope you enjoy reading it, walking it and immersing yourself in the curious combination of blood and beauty that is Midsomer. We have.

Martin Andrew, 2016

KEYS

WALK INFORMATION

 Dog friendliness

 Toilets

 Parking

 Eating

 Sat nav guide

 Map

KEY TO MAPS

 Gate

 Stile

 Kissing gate

 Pub

 Cafe

 Church

Point of interest

 Parking

Woodland

Hill

Foot bridge

Windmill

White Ducks and Witchert Walls

WALK 1 COPSES AND ROBBERS 4.5 MILES (7.2KM)

Brill

INTRODUCTION

Brill, a fine hilltop village on the western edge of Buckinghamshire, enjoys splendid sweeping views across the Oxfordshire clay vales and the Vale of Aylesbury. It is famed for its windmill, which in part dates from the 1680s and has been much photographed silhouetted against the sunset. The village itself is an attractive one, much of it built in brick and tiles produced from the hills on which it sits. We followed field paths and tracks, as well as some village roads in Brill and Oakley. The tracks, such as Span Green and that north of Oakley, can be muddy, sometimes with spectacular puddles in winter. Livestock is found on Brill Hill and some of the fields, Brill Hill having areas of good-quality grassland.

Because the route descends and ascends Brill Hill there is obviously some climbing but nothing too strenuous, even though Oakley is about 330ft (100m) lower than Brill's village centre. Brill's height ensures some impressive views.

 Much of the route is dog friendly but the pasture fields may be being grazed when you walk the route. In Oakley and Brill dogs should be on leads.

 No public toilets so rely on those in the pubs in Brill.

 Park near The Pointer pub near the church green.

 The Pointer or The Pheasant in Brill.

 The Pointer, Brill, HP18 9RT.

 Ordnance Survey Explorer 180.

MIDSOMER COMES TO BRILL

For *Midsomer Murders* fans, **Brill** featured in 'A Tale of Two Hamlets' while the village centre with its green and the former Wesleyan chapel of 1842, the parish church and The Pointer pub/restaurant all had starring roles in 'Four Funerals and a Wedding' with the former Wesleyan chapel becoming Pankhurst Hall. Until its recent makeover and renaming as The Pointer, the former Red Lion became The John Knox for *Midsomer* purposes.

A BIT OF HISTORICAL BACKGROUND

Brill was the centre of the Bernwood Forest, a royal forest from at least the time of the eleventh-century king, Edward the Confessor, who built a hunting lodge at Brill. Eventually, in the early 1630s, the forest was sold off or 'de-forested' by an impecunious King Charles I. Its extent included the parishes of Brill, Oakley and Boarstall. A beautiful coloured map of the area still survives, made for New College, Oxford, in 1591 with the intention of proving an obscure point in a lawsuit.

Brill Mill.

The hedges may not have been protected but the stile is.

Although Brill had a royal hunting lodge from the mid-eleventh century and it was from here that the entire Bernwood Forest was administered, its church was merely a chapelry or dependent church to Oakley. Oakley, meanwhile, remained a small village, jealous of the rights of its church over that of Brill. Oakley must have watched with envy as Brill became a medieval market town, complete with mills, market and fair, clay pits and even a prison: a bustling hilltop town with royal patronage and indeed occasional residence. However, by the mid-fourteenth century, kings and their courtiers shifted their allegiance mainly to Woodstock and the town declined. Its market town nature is very clear in its layout and buildings but from the seventeenth century it had to rely on brick making and agriculture in the deforested fields.

Our walk takes place entirely within the boundaries of the Bernwood Forest with many of the gently curving hedge boundaries that we pass through and alongside dating from the mid-seventeenth century after the sell-off.

THE WALK

1. We set off on a blustery day in early March from The Green, parking near The Pointer pub and walked west towards The Square, actually another green with a telephone box and the village's war memorial cross.

The village has a fine mix of red-brick houses and cottages with occasional accents of local limestone and the toffee-coloured Greensand stone but brick is what you would expect here. Brill Hill, as you will shortly see, is pockmarked and pitted with hollows and depressions that were formed by clay digging for the famous Brill bricks and roof tiles. It is said that the cottages were built with rejects from the numerous small brickworks, higher-class houses having used some of the first-rate ones, the rest being sold elsewhere.

Even so, if you look carefully you will see that the seventeenth to nineteenth-century brick is often a veneer on older timber-framed houses and cottages. At The Square we bore right along the High Street, passing Bernwode House, a good example of local virtuoso bricklaying of the 1770s with a barometer set in its garden wall, here a plaque records that it was given to Brill by Sir Edmund Verney of nearby Claydon House in 1910.

2. At Windmill Street we turned left and, just beyond The Pheasant pub, bore left along a small lane to descend past the famous windmill. Still working well into the twentieth century, it is a post mill with elements dating back to the 1680s and presides over an extensive landscape; the hills in the foreground pitted with old brick clay diggings, now carpeted in turf cropped by sheep or Dexter cattle, the vale of Oxfordshire beyond. Further along the lane we continued ahead where the tarmac ends, soon bearing right just past Old Farm to a stile.

Over this stile we headed downhill, now in pasture enclosed from the forest by straight hedges after the 1630s. Passing through the hedge via another stile, set in splendid isolation in a wide hedge gap, we headed a quarter right towards another stile. Over this the path is clear through the field ahead and we continued downhill to cross a small stream, one of many springing from the slopes of Brill Hill, this one

The Pointer, then known as The Red Lion, had starring roles in 'Four Funerals and a Wedding'. It was The John Knox for Midsomer Murders *purposes.*

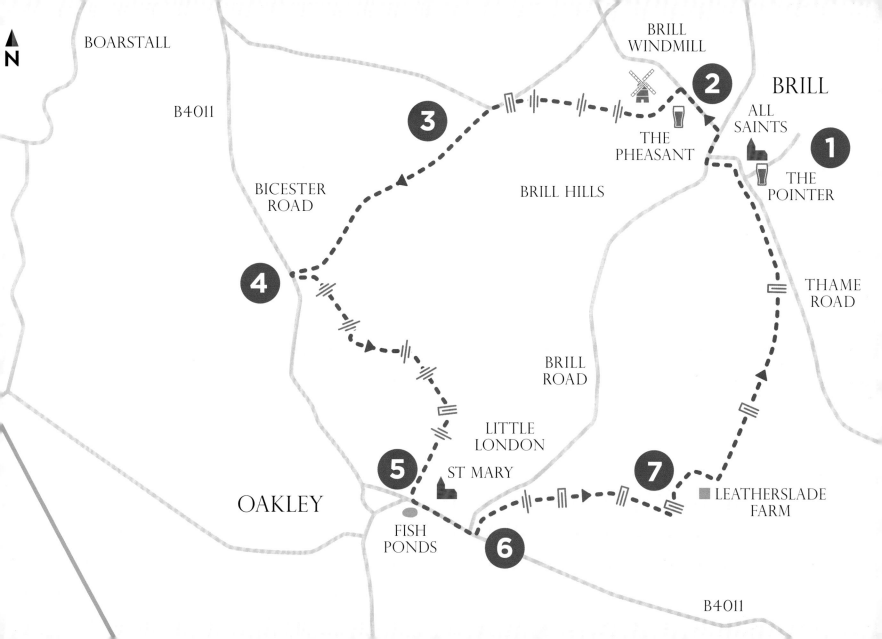

eventually joining the River Thame at Worminghall. We bore half left to a kissing gate and through this the path meanders amid trees to a road, the one from Brill to the deserted medieval village of Boarstall. It has the remains of a fine moated manor house and is famous for having the earliest map of a Buckinghamshire village, dating from the 1440s.

3. We turned left along this road and at Touchbridge, a seventeenth and eighteenth-century farmhouse with its sash windows prettily painted white with green frames, we continued ahead along a green lane, locally called Span Green and wide enough for sheep to graze the margins. This is an un-tarmacked section of the old road from Wotton Underwood to Oakley that skirted the foot of Brill Hill. In winter this lane can be muddy and deeply rutted but at least it is traffic-free, although on this early March day it was pretty hard going in places.

4. After about two thirds of a mile we reached a fork in the path, now within earshot of the busy Thame to Bicester road. We took the left fork and after fifty paces went left again to a stile. Over this we crossed a pasture field diagonally to its corner. Traversing the stile we went sharp right along the edge of an arable field, then shortly right, through a hedge gap, on to a hedged green lane. Again this can be pretty muddy and puddly in winter. The green lane soon bearing left, we continued along it for about 250yds, leaving it to go right over a stile. We were now in a narrow field, formerly part of Oakley's medieval open fields but enclosed in the seventeenth century. In these fields the enclosure hedges followed the edges

A view from Brill to Oakley.

of the curved ploughed groups of strips that produced corrugated fields of 'ridge and furrow' so beloved of landscape historians.

Over another stile we continued to the banks of a stream, descended to cross it, before heading towards a kissing gate in the hedge ahead. Here we turned right to rejoin the green lane and continue down it to emerge past Nap Farm on to the main road in Oakley.

5. Opposite are the medieval fishponds of the manor but we turned left along the pavement to visit the church in Oakley, whose name means a clearing in the oak woods: a fitting name for one of the main settlements within the Bernwood Forest. Continuing past Church Cottages, whose seventeenth-century timber-frame skeleton is just visible on the facade, we bore left into Brill Road and the hamlet of Little London, which in true *Midsomer Murders* style was the scene of a real-life shotgun murder in the 1990s.

6. We walked along the lane and, opposite Little London Farm, crossed a stile to head half left across pasture to a smart metal kissing gate. Through this we crossed the next field to a field gate and continued ahead, gently uphill, to reach another kissing gate well to the right of a house. Through the gate we turned left on to the track that passes the notorious Leatherslade Farm.

7. Leatherslade Farm achieved notoriety as the hideout of the Great Train Robbers who bought it in summer 1963. From here they drove to nearby Leighton Buzzard and on 8 August stopped and robbed the mail train of £2.5 million in bank notes. It was a sensational crime at the time but their incompetence meant that they were captured after failing to clean up the farm properly before scarpering. The rest, as they say, is history. They have seldom been out of sight with numerous films, memoirs and books on the subject. The train driver, meanwhile, never really recovered from the violent assault inflicted on him.

However, of the 1960s Leatherslade Farm nothing remains and a new house occupies its site. The walk weaves northwards along the green lane, past the farm and uphill to a field gate. Through this we continued in sheep pasture alongside the right-hand hedge as far as another field gate with a pair of cottages beyond. Here we reached the road and turned left to walk back into Brill and the end of the walk.

WALK 2   FLOOD LANDS OF THE RIVER THAME   4.5 MILES (7.2KM)

*Chearsley, **Cuddington** and Nether Winchendon*

INTRODUCTION

This route traverses field paths, tracks and village roads. The river can flood in winter and sections may well be muddy but livestock is only found in the pastures along the route and then not always.

Generally easy going with gentle ascents and descents to cross the Thame Valley.

MIDSOMER COMES TO THE VILLAGES ALONG THE RIVER THAME

The walk starts at The Bell pub in Chearsley at the west end of the village and where in earlier days much trade was picked up from travellers along the route from

 Dog friendly, but keep dogs on a lead in fields with animals and on village streets.

 No public toilets so rely on those in the two pubs en route.

 Park near The Bell in Chearsley.

 The Crown in Cuddington or The Bell in Chearsley.

 The Bell Inn, HP18 0DJ.

 Ordnance Survey Explorer 180 and 181.

'Death and Dreams' features Tibby's Cottage.

Aylesbury to Long Crendon and beyond. It became The Woodman and the village stores opposite became Elverton Village Stores and Post Office in 'Country Matters'.

Lower Winchendon church, Blenheim Cottage nearby and Nether Winchendon House all feature on the walk. Scenes were shot here for various episodes, including 'Things That Go Bump in the Night' and 'Death in Disguise', Nether Winchendon House becoming the Lodge of Golden Windhorse in 'Death in Disguise'.

Cuddington, however, has provided most locations to date of the three villages with The Crown, the parish church, Bernard Hall, the village shop, Tyringham Hall and Tibby's Cottage all used in various episodes, including 'Death in Disguise' again, 'Bad Tidings', 'Talking to the Dead', 'Death of a Stranger', 'Things That Go Bump in the Night', 'Shot at Dawn' and 'Death and Dreams'.

Quite a shooting list for three villages on a 4.5-mile walk!

A BIT OF HISTORICAL BACKGROUND

Of these three pretty villages, Chearsley and Lower Winchendon are on the north banks of the notoriously flood-prone River Thame while the other, Cuddington, is uphill to the south, growing up around springs and a stream that feeds north into the Thame.

Yet the villages are very different in character, particularly Chearsley, which grew up a maze of complicated and secretive lanes running from the north-east to south-west road on the ridge downhill almost to the river itself. Newcomers always find the village confusing. Lower Winchendon has widely spaced houses with a sort of focus around the church while Cuddington has a rectangle of streets and a more coherent plan.

All three villages retain their medieval churches and each is well worth visiting. Our favourite is Nether Winchendon, which keeps the atmosphere in its nave of an unrestored medieval church converted for Georgian worship. Each village has good houses and cottages from Tudor to nineteenth-century times, and there is a range of building materials, from timber-framing to stone via witchert, the earth wall construction found in the villages of the Thame Valley. Witchert, a local dialect word, is talked about in more detail in Walk 3, which is based in Haddenham, known as the 'capital' of the witchert country.

The route takes in the best of these villages and their settings, crossing and re-crossing the Thame. The walk passes over ridge and furrow in places, those distinctive corrugations that were produced by medieval and later plough teams when the fields of the villages were farmed in common. The soil was piled up in ridges while the furrows assisted drainage and, after the common fields were enclosed (Chearsley's by Act of Parliament in 1763), ridge and furrow survived where the new owners converted closes (or fields) to animal husbandry. Grass grew over the old ploughings and thus preserved them for posterity under a thick layer of turf. Ridge and furrow, as it's called, is one of the most exciting survivals in our countryside as it allows you to reconstruct in your mind's eye what the landscape looked like when medieval or Tudor peasants toiled behind their ploughs and before modern fields were formed.

THE WALK

1. On a somewhat overcast day in September we set off from The Bell pub at the north end of Chearsley village and headed right to go downhill past White Cottage, then down the lane called Watts Green. We continued left into Dark Lane, still heading downhill.

At the Y-junction with Elm Brook Close we went left on to a footpath past Long Meadow, an old barn converted into a house, leaving the village behind and continued to the end of the path.

2. Here we bore left alongside a fence to go through a bridle gate, then shortly over a stile. Now in a large arable field, we continued ahead alongside the hedge, following the Bernwood Jubilee Way, one of numerous way-marked paths in this area. Leaving the field over another stile, we bore a quarter left across pasture, following a shallow holloway, part of the medieval track to Lower Winchendon, the village we were now heading towards. We continued ahead at a cross path towards an electricity pole and climbed a stile in the hedge to reach the Cuddington to Chearsley road.

Nether Winchendon House, the Lodge of Golden Windhorse in 'Death in Disguise'.

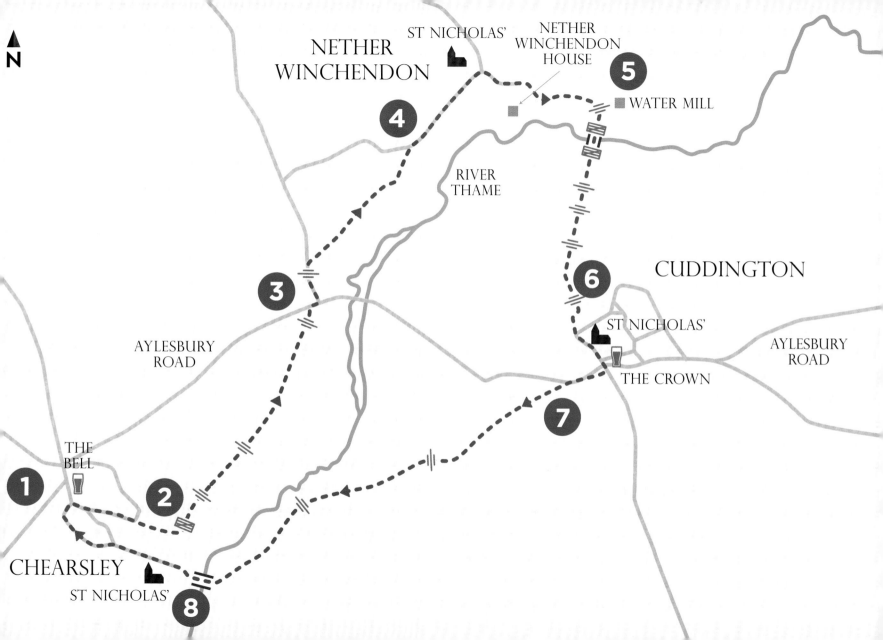

3. We crossed the road and bore right to the T-junction where we went left. Shortly afterwards we left the road, going right across a stile. We continued ahead across a cultivated field heading for a grass strip alongside a hedge, next bearing left towards a timber-framed house and passed through the hedge on to the village road in Lower Winchendon.

4. The timber-framed house is The Old Parsonage; the date 1676 appears in the dormer gable and refers to the modernisation, by the then parson, of an older early seventeenth-century house. We turned right along the lane that winds through this scattered village to visit the quite delightful parish church of St Nicholas, which has local stone setts in the tower, known locally as 'pitchings', and old quarry tiles on the nave floor. It also, somewhat unusually, retains all of its Georgian box pews, west gallery and Jacobean three-decker pulpit. Behind the church is the very large timber-framed manor house, which dates from Tudor and Stuart times.

From the church we went past the postbox set in its circular stone enclosure with a ball finial that in fact dates from the 1920s, and then down the lane past Blenheim Cottage, which featured in 'Death in Disguise'. Shortly we passed the brick stables and coach house to Nether Winchendon House, then past its gates with views of the house itself at the end of its tree-lined drive. The lane continues as far as the old watermill with its attached early nineteenth-century miller's house. The watermill bays are now converted as part of the house.

5. We bore right at the mill house to a stile, continuing ahead alongside willow trees and a hedge to cross the River Thame via a footbridge with hand gates at each end. We continued in pasture alongside more willow trees and a hedge to cross two stiles and walked between the hedge and a fence, the pasture on the right corrugated with old ridge and furrow. Over another stile the path climbs alongside a willow-girt and hedged stream, the field now arable.

6. At the field corner we went through a gate and across a footbridge/dam with a duck pond with many ducks on the right. Bearing right we walked along a lane, Tibby's Lane, past the picture postcard Tibby's Cottage up to the village of Cuddington. Turning right we followed the lane, curving around the churchyard of St Nicholas parish church with the village school on the right, then past the Bernard Hall, which was built for the village in the 1930s by the Bernards of Nether Winchendon House. The church is often locked but is well worth a visit with its fine thirteenth-century nave arcades.

Reaching the crossroads with the Aylesbury to Chearsley Road, we had lunch in The Crown before heading west out of the village, past the small green with its old iron communal water pump. After The Old Inn we crossed the road to a track just before the derestriction sign and by the fittingly named Bridleway Cottage.

7. We followed this bridleway out of the village, allotments to our left. At the end of the bridleway we passed through a kissing gate and continued ahead across ancient ridge and furrow towards a field gate. We passed through the hedge and crossed the field diagonally, again the pasture corrugated with ridge and furrow, to another stile. Over this we walked alongside a hedge, then ahead as a fence bears left. We headed towards the footbridge across the River Thame.

8. Over the footbridge we aimed for Chearsley church tower and passed through a kissing gate to continue up a path to reach a village lane. Now back in Chearsley, we followed the lane to the parish church of St Nicholas. Curiously, all three medieval parish churches in the villages on this walk are dedicated to St Nicholas.

Inside the church the chancel arch is very much offset as the chancel was rebuilt on a different axis and, as at Lower Winchendon, there is a west gallery lit by windows high up the nave walls. These illuminate also a nave roof in which each medieval tie beam supports different and altered beams above, while on the wall is a copy of a map of the parish made in 1763. This shows all the old field boundaries and their names just before the parish was enclosed and the modern field pattern superimposed.

We left this interesting church set at the east end of the village and well down the hill. Immediately to its east is a moated site, which was the location of the original but long-gone manor house. Presumably the church was built for the convenience of the lord of the manor rather than the parishioners, but ironically the church has long outlasted the manor house.

From the church we continued along this lane, passing a reed-filled rectangular pond, probably used for washing the villagers' clothes and later provided with a cast-iron water pump. At a Y-junction we bore left up Church Lane and back to The Bell for refreshment.

The Bell, which became The Woodman in 'Country Matters'.

Slowly flows the River Thame.

Cuddington Village was used in various episodes, including 'Death in Disguise', 'Bad Tidings', 'Talking to the Dead', 'Death of a Stranger', 'Things That Go Bump in the Night', 'Shot at Dawn' and 'Death and Dreams'.

Blenheim Cottage, Nether Winchendon, was seen in various episodes, including 'Things That Go Bump in the Night' and 'Death in Disguise'.

Nether Winchendon postbox.

19

ANCIENT WALLS, RIDGES AND ENCLOSURES 6.75 MILES (10.9KM)

Haddenham and Dinton

INTRODUCTION

The walk starts and finishes in Haddenham, the 'capital' of the witchert country. 'Witchert', spelt in various ways, is the distinctive earth wall or 'cob' type of buildings and walls that give visitors a slight feeling of being in Devon or Dorset where cob buildings are common. It is a dialect corruption of 'white earth' and the route winds through this large and, like Long Crendon (Walk 4), historic village, then across country to Dinton and Westlington, also villages with witchert buildings. The route then heads south to the tiny village of Aston Sandford with its equally tiny church before returning to Haddenham. It is not a hilly walk but packed with interest as well as being the longest in the book.

The route includes two stretches of village roads and paths but the bulk of it is in open countryside, some arable and some pastoral. There are three parish churches, a couple of Nonconformist chapels in Haddenham and a lot of good historic cottages and farmhouses en route, as well as Dinton Hall, a grander type of country house.

MIDSOMER COMES TO HADDENHAM, DINTON AND WESTLINGTON

In July 2014, *Midsomer Murders* was filming on Haddenham (or should I say Midsomer Oaks) village green with Neil Dudgeon as DCI John Barnaby, John Nettles – or Tom's – cousin. Over the years Tom Barnaby and his sidekicks have used Haddenham in numerous episodes. The walk starts at the village green in Church End where the local Towersey Morris Men danced in 'Judgement Day'. The area around the green, with its fine medieval parish church, picturesque pond and collection of fine houses and cottages, has been seen in many other episodes. These include 'Birds of Prey', 'A Talent for Life', 'Vixen's Run', 'Midsomer Life' and 'Orchis Fatalis'. Top Barn, a house opposite Church Farmhouse, the fifteenth-century timber-framed house east of the church (also seen in *Midsomer Murders*),

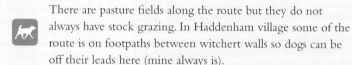

There are pasture fields along the route but they do not always have stock grazing. In Haddenham village some of the route is on footpaths between witchert walls so dogs can be off their leads here (mine always is).

No public toilets so rely on those in the pubs.

Park at Church End, near to the parish church in Haddenham.

We lunched at The Seven Stars in Dinton, which is excellent and was bought by the community to save it from closure. It now thrives with French chef Stephanie in charge. We also had a cappuccino in Little Italy at Fort End in Haddenham en route.

The postcode for Church Farmhouse, the timber-framed house by St Mary's church, in Haddenham is HP17 8AE.

Ordnance Survey Explorer 181.

was used in 'Things That Go Bump in the Night' with Elizabeth Key murdered in its front garden, while the butchers west of the green, featured in 'Birds of Prey': rather aptly as characters bought sausages there. The route through the village also passes another couple of locations that we will point out in the route description section.

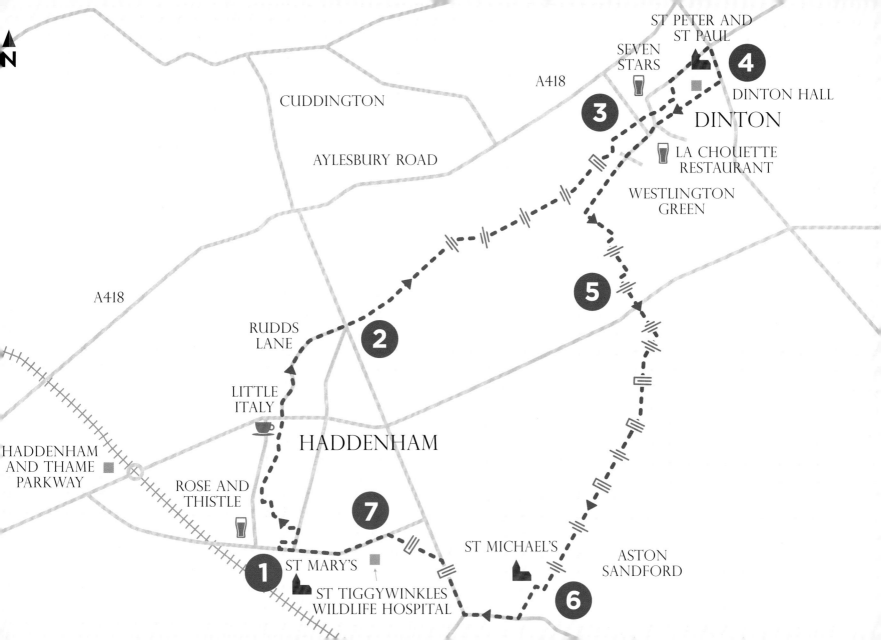

N

CUDDINGTON

AYLESBURY ROAD

A418

ST PETER AND
ST PAUL

SEVEN
STARS

3

4

DINTON HALL

DINTON

LA CHOUETTE
RESTAURANT

WESTLINGTON
GREEN

2

RUDDS
LANE

5

LITTLE
ITALY

HADDENHAM

HADDENHAM
AND THAME
PARKWAY

ROSE AND
THISTLE

7

ST MICHAEL'S

ASTON
SANDFORD

1

ST MARY'S

ST TIGGYWINKLES
WILDLIFE HOSPITAL

6

Dinton church featured in 'Who Killed Cock Robin?' for a wedding and Westlington's delightful thatched-cottage-girt village green had a macabre role when a body was found down a well, also in 'Who Killed Cock Robin?' The green was also used in 'Dead Letters', as was the nearby Belgian restaurant, La Chouette, which became the Hearts of Oak pub.

A BIT OF HISTORICAL BACKGROUND

Witchert is what sets Haddenham and a belt of villages running west from the Aylesbury area to Thame and beyond in Oxfordshire, apart from the other historic villages in Midsomer. Witchert or 'white earth' is the local lime-rich clay produced by the decay of the Portland limestone strata that runs beneath this area. In my garden in Haddenham I reach this clay at a depth of about a foot. Building with earth is a very ancient tradition used all over the world, from African mud huts and American pueblos to Devon and Dorset cob. Witchert is a remarkable vernacular material used only a little over 30 miles from London.

The Green Dragon, Haddenham.

Witchert is an ideal mix of binder (the clay) and aggregate (the small stones and limestone fragments within the clay). It can be used to produce high walls much thinner than is possible in Devon cob. I've seen walls a mere 9in thick at over 8ft high. These boundary walls and farm buildings generally appear without render, unlike the houses and cottages. The technique involves building a stone plinth, locally named a 'grumpling' and raising the cob in courses about 2ft high called 'berries', the cob is mixed with water and chopped straw to make it workable. In theory the walls should remain sturdy to a great height and a few buildings, many of them chapels, reach 30ft. The tops have to be protected either by copings, if walls, or roofs, if farm buildings, outbuildings or dwellings. If thus treated, witchert is very durable and there is evidence in the Vale of Aylesbury of witchert that is over 400 years old.

Witchert gives a distinctive and unusual character to this string of villages with their high rendered boundary walls curving and swooping between cottages and along winding narrow alleyways and paths and the numerous rendered cottages and houses. In this book you will see witchert on Walks 2, 3 and 4. Maintenance is a problem these days but every owner should remember this local saying (explaining how witchert walls decay if you let the roofs or copings fail or let the ground rise above the stone grumpling plinths): 'Give 'em a good hat and boots and they won't piss themselves.' Sound, if direct, advice!

THE WALK

1. The walk started at the village green in Haddenham's Church End on a sunny September day, racing fluffy clouds overhead. After visiting the church we headed north, away from the green and Churchway. On our right is what used to be The Green Dragon pub and briefly a wine bar dining establishment renamed 'Twist at the Green Dragon'. Opposite we bore left into Dragon Tail, a witchert-walled alley passing a sinuous topiary dragon. At the end we bore right into The Croft. After winding left and right we turned left into another witchert-walled alley which emerged by The King's Head pub. Here we turned right into the High Street and continued ahead, passing the Methodist church, also built in witchert, with Haddenham Museum behind it in the church's old Sunday school. Just before we reached the Little Italy cafe we passed a thatched cottage behind high walls, No. 2, which was in 'Orchis Fatalis' as Margaret Winstanley's house.

After an excellent coffee in Little Italy we crossed Fort End to pass to the right of the Cottage Bakery, now on the Outer Aylesbury Ring footpath, into Fern Lane. On the right, just before the witchert barn, No. 2 Fern Lane became Lady Annabel Butler's house in the 'Vixen's Run' episode. We continued ahead on another witchert wall-lined footpath alongside The Old Brewery and emerged on Townsend Green, another of Haddenham's small open spaces. We continued along Rudds Lane and passed a pond and the post office.

2. Here we crossed to a green lane bridleway with a guidepost stating that Dinton was 1.5 miles away. Initially metalled, the lane became a hedged path and continued ahead. Where the bridle path bore left we continued ahead to a kissing gate, now on the Wychert Way Link. We bore half right across pasture to a kissing gate, traces of medieval ridge and furrow corrugating the field. Past the

Church Farmhouse, the fifteenth-century timber-framed house east of the church, was used in 'Things That Go Bump in the Night'.

Parminters the Butchers, now the Egg House Butchery, featured in 'Birds of Prey'.

kissing gate we continued ahead alongside the hedge, then over a stile in a light wire fence, heading to a hand gate in the field corner. Through this we continued alongside the hedge to another hand gate. Alongside the hedge in a field with sheep grazing we headed to another hand gate. This led us into a pony paddock, which we crossed to another hand gate. Across more paddock we reached a lane, now on the edge of Westlington, via another hand gate.

We turned left, on the lane, then right through a kissing gate into a paddock and passed beneath a stand of horse-chestnut trees. Through another hand gate we crossed a smaller paddock to a path between fences, via another hand gate. The path emerged on a village road in Dinton and we crossed to The Seven Stars pub for an excellent lunch.

3. Leaving The Seven Stars we walked along the narrow lane at its side, at its end merging with a larger lane. Where this bore left we carried straight on up a no through road between cottages. At the end of this lane we turned left by a footpath sign on to a path, then through a kissing gate to reach a lane. Here we bore right along it to pass Dinton Hall, a large mainly sixteenth and seventeenth-century mansion with fine stone gate piers with ball finials and a large conical-roofed dovecote. Beyond we went into the churchyard of Saints Peter and Paul parish church, a fine medieval church but often locked, although you can admire the spectacular Norman south doorway of about 1140 from the outside. Richly ornamented, it has a lintel carved with St George slaying the dragon and a tree carved in the tympanum (the semicircular slab above the lintel). The tree is a representation of the Tree of Life and has a twelfth-century Latin inscription: 'If anyone despairs of having rewards for his merits let this man hear advice and let him retain it.'

Haddenham Green, a regular in Midsomer Murders.

4. We left via the south-east corner of the churchyard through a stone arch and descended past more massive stone gate piers to Dinton Hall as far as a footpath sign and bore right through a kissing gate. We walked alongside a fence with good views to our right of the south front of Dinton Hall, and long views over pasture towards the Chilterns on our left. We crossed a stream via two kissing gates and beyond these the path passed between gardens to reach a lane. Here we bore right past The Old Boot, a former pub, into the High Street.

Continuing ahead we passed La Chouette, a Belgian restaurant that has featured in a *Midsomer Murders* episode, 'Dead Letters', and then reached Westlington Green. Here we continued ahead into Westlington Lane, which becomes a track after leaving Westlington village. We continued alongside a hedge, an arable field to the left. Passing through a gap in a straggly hedge we bore left, keeping the hedge on our left to follow the ancient parish boundary between Dinton and Haddenham.

At the end of the pasture field we bore right briefly, then left through the hedge via a stile. Over this we continued ahead, still in pasture, alongside the hedge and out over a stile in a hedge at the end of the field.

5. We emerged on the 'low road' between Haddenham and Hartwell, and crossed it with care via another stile into more pasture, this one often grazed by cattle. Continuing south alongside a hedge, at a gap we bore half right into a meadow, over a fence. At a footpath post we went through another hedge gap and crossed a smallish field to a stile, a meandering reedy stream on our left. We headed to a bridge, Stokenchurch Telecom Tower dead ahead on the Chiltern ridge. We crossed the footbridge via a hand gate and a stile. In the pasture we skirted a medieval moated site, and headed for a stile in the hedge ahead. Over this we continued ahead across two arable fields via a footbridge between them, Aston Sandford ahead. Over a stile we crossed a pasture to another stile to the left of the church.

A witchert wall alleyway.

A dragon hedge.

6. Over the stile we visited the churchyard and, fortunately for us, the church was open. St Michael's parish church, with its weatherboarded bellcote, is small and, although in the main of thirteenth-century origin, was heavily restored in the 1870s. Its chief glory is probably the thirteenth-century stained glass in the middle light of the chancel east window. A rare survival, it shows a seated Christ holding a box of nard, an expensive aromatic oil or ointment used in the ritual anointing of hands, feet or foreheads.

Leaving the well-treed churchyard we turned right and then bore left, passing Aston Sandford Manor, which has a timber-framed north range and a grander Victorian Tudor south block designed by Sir George Gilbert Scott whose grandfather had been rector of Aston Sandford. It was built in 1867 by Robert Rose of the Haddenham Rose dynasty, a beam in the roof is inscribed 'ROBERT ROSE Builder Haddenham 1867'.

The lane reached a T-junction where we bore right and followed this road to the next T-junction where we again turned right to cross the stream that we had crossed earlier in the fields north-east of Aston Sandford and which joins the River Thame north-west of Thame. Over the bridge we bore left through a kissing gate and then immediately right to walk along the field side of the roadside hedge and passed through a hedge gap. Shortly, at a footpath sign, we bore half left across a field to a kissing gate and continued on the same bearing to another kissing gate to the right of modern farm buildings. Another kissing gate and we reached the road, Aston Road, which leads into Haddenham.

A welcoming coffee at Little Italy, Haddenham.

The Belgian restaurant, La Chouette, which became the Hearts of Oak in 'Dead Letters'.

7. We bore left and visited St Tiggywinkle's, the wild animal hospital founded and still run by the indefatigable Les Stocker and his family. There are numerous kites, hedgehogs, and other wild animals here as well as a cup of tea: it's always a popular outing with my grandchildren. Leaving it we continued left and back into the village and the end of the walk.

WALK 4 ACTORS AND OLD LACE 3.5 MILES (5.7KM)

Long Crendon

INTRODUCTION

The walk starts and finishes in the large and historic village of Long Crendon, which is at the south end of a limestone ridge about 40m above the valley of the meandering River Thame. From the village the route descends to the river valley and heads to Notley Abbey, notable for its medieval monastic remains, dovecote and great tithe barn. Once Lawrence Olivier and Vivien Leigh lived here and we also passed the evocative remains of Notley's watermill. Near it, on the far side of the river, cattle or sheep graze but you can easily avoid them.

The route takes in the heart of Long Crendon and descends to the mainly arable fields along the Thame Valley where navigation is pretty straightforward.

Long Crendon parish church and the fifteenth-century courthouse featured in 'Dead Letters' and 'Blood Wedding'.

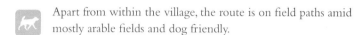 Apart from within the village, the route is on field paths amid mostly arable fields and dog friendly.

 No public toilets so rely on those in the pubs.

P Park in The Square (at the crossroads with Frogmore Lane, the High Street and the B4011 through road).

🍴 We lunched at The Flower Pot cafe in The Square: delightful. There are many other choices, including The Churchill Arms, which does Thai food, and the Eight Bells, both in the High Street.

SAT NAV The postcode for The Flower Pot cafe in The Square is HP18 9AA.

ⓞ Ordnance Survey Explorer 180.

MIDSOMER COMES TO LONG CRENDON (AGAIN AND AGAIN)

Long Crendon has been much loved as a location for *Midsomer Murders*, as has nearby Thame and Haddenham (Walk 3). Our walk started down Frogmore Lane and passed Long Crendon Manor, which is seen through the archway of its fifteenth-century stone gatehouse. It featured in numerous episodes including 'Death and Dreams', 'Things That Go Bump in the Night', 'Garden of Death', 'The Christmas Haunting' and 'Not in My Backyard'. Opposite is a cottage seen in 'Garden of Death'. Frogmore Lane itself was in 'A Tale of Two Hamlets' (as 'Lower Warden') and in 'Second Sight'. The superb High Street has similarly been used frequently in episodes, including 'Garden of Death', 'Blood on the Saddle', 'Blood Wedding', 'Tainted Fruit' and 'The House in the Woods'. Buildings seen include The Eight Bells pub, Madges, Tudor Cottage (No. 29), Primrose Cottage, the Long Crendon Community Library and the Church House, which became 'Midsomer District Council Library' in 'Blood Wedding'. At the east end of the High Street the parish church and the fifteenth-century courthouse featured in 'Dead Letters' and 'Blood Wedding', the latter owned by the National Trust and open at certain times. Near and to the left of the courthouse is a somewhat uninspiring Edwardian red-brick house, Old College Farmhouse, which was used as the Goodings' house in 'Dead Letters'.

A BIT OF HISTORICAL BACKGROUND

Long Crendon and Haddenham (Walk 3) hung on to their medieval open field farming until well into the nineteenth century, Long Crendon's Enclosure Act dating from 1824 and Haddenham's from 1830. This meant that they were villages of middling and small tenant farmers cultivating the surrounding fields in common, many of these old houses and cottages survive within the village, often with medieval timber frames. Long Crendon has over twenty houses with cruck frames – that is heavy A-frames that divide the building into bays and which pre-date the reign of Henry VIII – as well as sixteenth and seventeenth-century more normal timber-framed houses. Much like Haddenham and a number of other villages in the area, it has witchert (earth-walled) houses and cottages as well as stone and brick ones. Haddenham would have had a similar number of cruck houses if disastrous fires in the eighteenth century had not intervened: as it is only three have survived.

Long Crendon's farmers and farm labourers eked out their incomes via their wives and daughters who took up lace making, particularly in the eighteenth and nineteenth centuries. From the seventeenth century needle making had served a similar function. Unfortunately machine-made lace and factory-made needles killed off both of these valuable sources of extra income by 1900.

Notley Abbey Woods.

Notley Abbey (Point 5) was founded in around 1160 by Walter Giffard, Earl of Buckingham, in his deer park east of the village near the banks of the River Thame (*parcus bestiarum silvaticarum*). Founding abbeys in former hunting parks was a bit of a vogue at the time as it made a ready-made 'desert' well away from settlements and with its own park pale (or boundary fence). The monks were Augustinians, as they were at Dorchester Abbey (Walk 16), and the church was a very long one by the time building was complete in the fourteenth century, standing at about 240ft (73m). It was a wealthy abbey but after the Dissolution in 1538 (under the ungrateful Henry VIII who had been a guest in the 1520s) it became a quarry and the plan of the church and much of the abbey was only revealed following excavation in the 1930s. The abbot's lodging or house does survive (it became a farmhouse) and also parts of the cloister walls. To the west the abbey's tithe barn and dovecote are passed on the route.

However, the abbey's main claim to fame is the years when Laurence Olivier and Vivien Leigh lived here (1944–58) and many stars of stage and screen visited them here, including Marlene Dietrich, Judy Garland, Marilyn Monroe, Katherine Hepburn and many, many more. The abbot's lodgings date from the fifteenth and early sixteenth century and it is fortunate that they survived as they are of high architectural quality. Olivier once described it as his favourite house and 'absolutely charming … it enchanted me'.

The scale of Long Crendon's fine parish church owes much to Notley Abbey as it was granted to the abbey along with other churches, including Ashenden, Chilton, Dorton and Lower Winchendon (Walk 2), and several further afield, such as Princes Risborough (Walk 7). These churches were part of the abbey's endowment but they had responsibilities for maintenance and providing a priest. It is a fine cruciform church with a tall central tower, some notable seventeenth-century timber screens enriched with Doric pilasters and turned balusters. The highlight is the splendid Dormer monument in the south transept, with a profusion of columns, arches, pinnacles and coats of arms on shields: a splendid 1620s example and with much now picked out in colour.

THE WALK

Site of the old watermill, River Thame.

1. Clear April sunshine and racing clouds accompanied us as we set off from The Square to walk down Frogmore Lane (it used to be called Frog Lane but that did not sound grand enough to the village's twentieth-century inhabitants). We passed Long Crendon Manor, glimpsing its timber-framed walls through the fifteenth-century stone archway in the gatehouse. Opposite is Cripps Cottage, which has also featured in *Midsomer Murders*. A little further downhill we bore right at a footpath sign, to follow the path that goes to the left of the quaintly named '4d Cottage': presumably its rent had at some stage been four old pence. The path ascended between gardens, then became a lane.

At the end we bore left past Hazel Cottage and crossed the main road, passing the war memorial and continuing into Chearsley Road, with playing fields to the right where both of us had played cricket when we were younger. We passed the Roman Catholic church of 1971 in an interesting modern style and well worth a look. We continued ahead and crossed Burts Lane.

2. Reaching the sign for the Eight Bells pub and the footpath waymark we turned right and passed through the pub yard where a game of Aunt Sally was under way. Through a passage between the pub and its neighbouring house we reached the High Street where we turned left, passing 'Madges' which was used for a murder in 'Blood on the Saddle'. The courthouse was not open but we visited the church, which was.

3. After visiting St Mary's church, which is most rewarding both for its monuments and Jacobean timber screens as well as the medieval parts, we retraced our steps a bit to turn left down a lane flanked by fine hedges at the footpath post, signed the Bernwood Jubilee Way and also the Thame Valley Walk. We continued past the gates of the manor house, actually built as a farmhouse in about 1700, and continued on the path to the right of a house called Game Keep. We descended between garden fences and then a paddock to emerge in pasture.

We followed the clear path ahead to the far corner of the field, went through the hedge gap and turned left before walking alongside a field drainage ditch with a hedge beyond, an arable field to the right. At a path junction we continued ahead past a guidepost, the hedge still on our left.

4. Reaching a footbridge and crossing a stile we bore a quarter left to continue on the Bernwood Jubilee Way and walked alongside a post and wire fence uphill

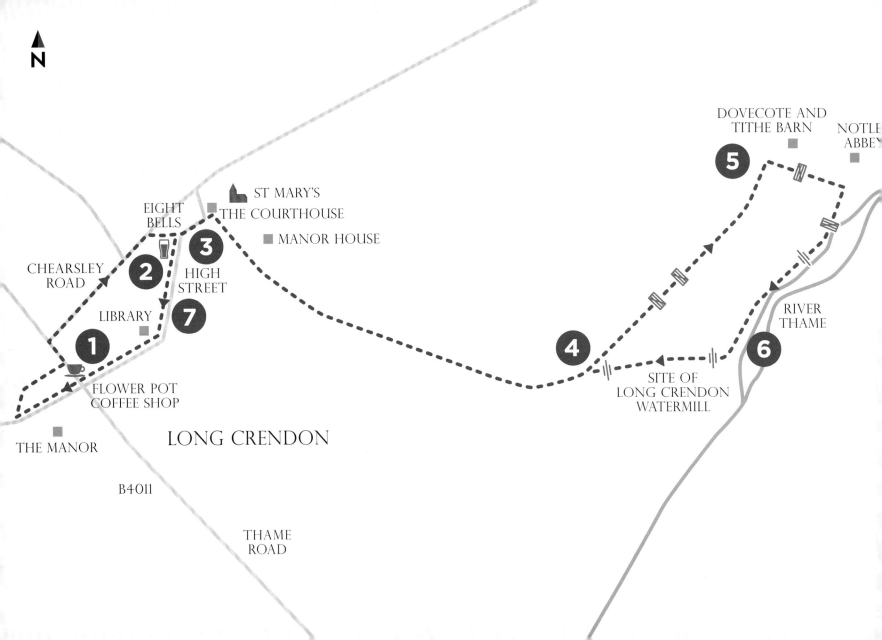

N

DOVECOTE AND
TITHE BARN

NOTLEY
ABBEY

5

ST MARY'S
EIGHT
BELLS
THE COURTHOUSE

MANOR HOUSE

CHEARSLEY
ROAD

2

3

HIGH
STREET

7

LIBRARY

1

RIVER
THAME

4

6

FLOWER POT
COFFEE SHOP

SITE OF
LONG CRENDON
WATERMILL

THE MANOR

LONG CRENDON

B4011

THAME
ROAD

towards the corner of a copse. We continued on the track past the end of the copse via two field gates, then alongside further post and wire fencing. We passed alongside modern farm buildings, now on a metalled track. At the Notley Tythe Barn sign we bore right, the medieval cruck tithe barn on our left, now a wedding and event venue. Beyond the barn complex we could see the pyramidal roof of the sixteenth-century stone dovecote. Astonishingly it has over 5,000 nest boxes set into the walls.

We headed for a hand gate beside the drive, now on the Wychert Way, to follow the path between fences with glimpses of Notley Abbey on the left, although filtered through hedges and trees.

5. What survives of Notley Abbey is mainly the abbot's lodgings and part of the west range of the monks' cloister, all in mellow stone. We followed the pretty path with bluebells in the margins in April as it curved away from the abbey to pass through another hand gate. We headed to the next hand gate, now on the Thame Valley Walk, as well as the Wychert Way. We headed along the grassy track beside a post and rail fence to a stile. Over this we continued ahead, the River Thame within the copse to our left.

Long Crendon Manor featured in numerous episodes, including 'Death and Dreams', 'Things That Go Bump in the Night', 'Garden of Death', 'The Christmas Haunting' and 'Not in My Backyard'.

6. At the next stile we crossed to look at the remains of Long Crendon or Notley Mill with its low walls, cart bridge and the brick-sided sluice way. It is a watermill archaeologist's delight, with sheep pottering about in the copse between the river proper and the millstream. The mill is mentioned in the Domesday Book of 1087 and continued to work into the 1930s, after which it was demolished to the ground.

We re-crossed the stile and headed half left across the arable field, Long Crendon ahead on its ridge. Back at the stile (Point 3) we re-crossed it and the footbridge to retrace our steps along the paths back into Long Crendon, and back up the lane to emerge near the courthouse once more. We turned left to retrace our steps along the High Street, passing the Eight Bells.

7. Beyond, where the road widens into a triangular area, is the Church House on the south side and Tudor Cottage on the north side, both featuring in *Midsomer Murders* episodes. We continued along the High Street, passing the Long Crendon Community Library, and reached the main road and The Square for lunch in The Flower Pot cafe.

A nice cake in the Long Crendon coffee shop.

The superb High Street has been used frequently, including in 'Garden of Death', 'Blood on the Saddle', 'Blood Wedding', 'Tainted Fruit' and 'The House in the Woods'.

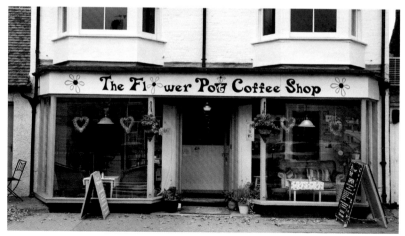

The Flower Pot Coffee Shop.

WALK 5 CHÂTEAU ROTHSCHILD 3 MILES (4.8KM)

Waddesdon Manor

INTRODUCTION

Waddesdon Manor is almost as famous for the Rothschilds transformation of a bare Buckinghamshire hill into a fully wooded one with vast, mature trees, as it is for the mansion. The hill in question is Lodge Hill, which rises some 200ft (60m) from the fields of the Vale of Aylesbury, and it was here that teams of horses hauled enormous trees with gigantic root balls from all over the country to form an instant forest. Waddesdon Manor and its parkland, all focusing on a mellow Bath stone French-style château, is very much the focus of this walk. The house is a National Trust property and its grounds are open to the public. The house, grounds and other features, such as the aviary, are richly rewarding and refreshments are also available here.

The route starts in Waddesdon village and, after visiting the unexpectedly grand parish church, heads west through attractive open countryside, the tree-covered Lodge Hill to our left, before heading south-east near Westcott, soon entering parkland skirting the lower slopes to Waddesdon Manor's hill. Entering the grounds we cross their south-east section, with an option to leave the route and head uphill to visit the manor. Leaving the grounds the route crosses pasture back to Waddesdon village.

MIDSOMER COMES TO WADDESDON MANOR

Waddesdon Manor was designed in the 1870s for Baron Ferdinand de Rothschild of that great pan-European banking family. He employed the splendidly named French architect Hippolyte Alexandre Gabriel Walter Destailleur. The style is unashamedly French Loire-château and what more natural than using its flamboyantly French architecture set down on a Buckinghamshire hill as a French location for *Midsomer Murders*? So Barnaby, ostensibly on holiday in

 The route is dog friendly but cattle graze some of the fields west of Lodge Hill.

 No public toilets, so rely on those in the pub en route or if you divert to Waddesdon Manor where there are toilets as well as refreshments.

 Park on the High Street in Waddesdon village.

 If you climb the hill from the route or visit Waddesdon Manor later, you can eat in the same restaurant as Barnaby did in 'Death of a Stranger'. Alternatively, in Waddesdon village we ate in The Lion on the High Street, which was good and welcoming. Near the church there is also The Long Dog (a dachshund) or opposite is The Five Arrows Hotel if you fancy something a bit posher.

 The postcode for The Lion pub in Waddesdon High Street is HP18 0LB.

 Ordnance Survey Explorer 181.

France, had a meal in the restaurant with his family in 'Death of a Stranger'. Other parts of the mansion and grounds appeared in this episode, still supposedly in France.

When Baron Ferdinand de Rothschild first saw Lodge Hill it was virtually treeless, an outlier from the Brill–Winchendon Hills, but he recognised its potential. Several of his uncles and cousins established themselves in existing or new country houses and estates in Buckinghamshire, some before him, others at the same time or soon after: Meyer at Mentmore and Sir Anthony at Aston Clinton and his cousins Nathan at Tring, just in Hertfordshire, Alfred at Halton, and Leopold at Ascott. Building started at Waddesdon in 1874 and continued until 1883 on the newly flattened hilltop. At the same time the mature woodland was created on and around the slopes of the hill and parkland was laid out.

Waddesdon Manor fountain.

Waddesdon Manor gardens.

Hippolyte Destailleur, for short, produced an extraordinary Loire château in the heart of Buckinghamshire with elements of such great French châteaux as Chambord, Chaumont and Blois. Its romantic skyline of turrets, conical and pyramidal towers and iron finials is quite unforgettable, as is the interior with its salvaged French furnishings, reusing panelling, mirrors and fireplaces, many from Paris; not to mention the superb porcelain and other collections on display.

The grounds are no less interesting with their winding paths and parterres flanked by numerous eighteenth-century statues (or copies) of Classical figures and, a favourite with my children, the aviary of 1889, still with birds amid its foliage.

It is inevitable that you will revisit this astonishing and wonderful house and, if you have not been before, this walk is only a taster: a full day is needed to really appreciate the house, its spectacular interior and the marvellous grounds.

THE WALK

1. On a sunny June day with high fluffy clouds we walked west along Waddesdon's High Street, passing Waddesdon Village Hall of 1897 and The Five Arrows Hotel of 1887, two of the many buildings and houses in the village built by the Rothschilds. The architect usually employed for these works was William Taylor of Bierton, a village just east of Aylesbury; Taylor was trained by George Devey, who Leopold Rothschild employed at Ascott. The emblem of a hand with five arrows appears on the hotel and other estate houses in the village; it is the badge of the Rothschilds – each arrow representing one of the sons of Mayer Amschel Rothschild, the founding father of the dynasty – and also became the name of the hotel. Beyond the war memorial cross we bore right and through a lychgate to visit the parish church of St Michael and All Angels with its long and wide six-bay nave. Four bays of the arcades into the south aisle and the reset south doorway are the most interesting elements architecturally, being late

A nice piece of Waddesdon Manor terracotta.

Waddesdon Manor in the trees.

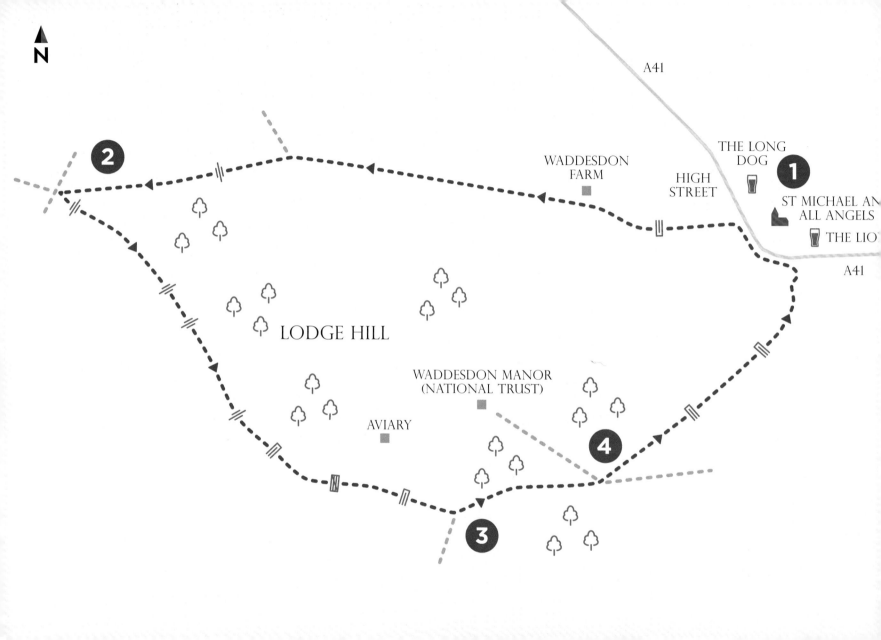

N

A41

THE LONG
DOG

WADDESDON
FARM

HIGH
STREET

1

ST MICHAEL AN
ALL ANGELS

THE LIO

A41

2

LODGE HILL

WADDESDON MANOR
(NATIONAL TRUST)

AVIARY

4

3

The Rothschilds' coat of arms: five arrows held by a hand.

Waddesdon Manor footpath post.

Norman to Transitional Gothic (that is mainly Norman but with pointed Gothic arches), all of about 1185 and sumptuous with scalloped capitals, colonettes and the south doorway with chevron of a late and complex pattern. Mind you, this robust late Norman work contrasts unfavourably for some people with the elegant simplicity of the rest of the nave, which is largely fourteenth century, but not so for dedicated fans of Anglo-Norman architecture like us.

From the porch we bore right to leave through the churchyard gate and passed The Long Dog pub; this was formerly The Bell and, like the church, it long pre-dated the Rothschilds' arrival, being partly seventeenth century. We crossed the main road into Queen Street, signposted The Dairy and Estate Yard, and walked past Rothschild estate cottages, one with a terracotta plaque of a hay wain on its gable, then the Waddesdon estate offices with a thatched octagonal dovecote in the centre of the yard (this was the estate dairy). Here we took a right fork and continued ahead through a kissing gate, still on tarmac, the walled former kitchen garden to Waddesdon Manor on our left. At the end of the wall our route merged with a metalled track to continue ahead, soon becoming a grassy one. To the north we had views to Quainton and its windmill (Walk 21). On our left was pretty pasture on the lower slopes of Lodge Hill.

At a footpath post we continued ahead across an arable field, passing through a hedge via a footbridge and stile into cattle pasture. We bore half right across to the corner of the field to a stile.

2. Over the stile we turned left and walked alongside the hedge, then over a double stile either side of a footbridge to continue alongside the hedge to another double stile and footbridge. Continuing alongside the hedge we climbed gently across Lodge Hill's lower slopes, Ashendon and Brill (Walk 1) on their hills away to our right. Through a kissing gate we continued ahead, now in uneven parkland cattle pasture. We head towards woodland and, breasting the steepish slope, headed for a hand gate close to the woodland edge. Through this we continued ahead, now close alongside Waddesdon Manor's woodland, and descended to a kissing gate and a footbridge. Over these we walked along the edge of an arable field running up a dry valley and we soon merged with a path coming from the right up this valley.

3. Here we turned left into Waddesdon Manor's park and woodland, now on the (Brill) Tramway Trail (Walk 21) and passed through woodland to reach the main access drive to the manor, amid lots of specimen conifers. Here we turned right along it with numerous magnificent pines and cedars on each side.

If a National Trust member you can go left at signs to the manor and follow the path uphill, as we did, the manor coming into view with its magnificent garden front and parterres. After the visit we retraced our steps downhill to pick up the drive where we had left it and continued along it, fine copper beeches and limes on our left.

4. At a footpath post we bore half left on to a path through grassy parkland, the path curving with huge Wellingtonias to our left, until we reached a kissing gate. Through this we continued across pasture to another kissing gate. The path entered a dark copse, soon crossed a drive into more woodland and bore left into a garage court to pass more Rothschild estate cottages (Nos 97 and 95) to emerge near the war memorial cross. We bore right into the High Street and repaired to The Lion for lunch, a beer and the end of the walk.

Waddesdon Manor on top of Lodge Hill.

THE RIDGEWAY NATIONAL TRAIL

WALK 6 LIONS AND A SPACE COWBOY 4.25 MILES (6.8KM)

Bledlow and Horsenden

INTRODUCTION

Our route climbs towards the Chiltern escarpment, but turns on to the Ridgeway National Trail after a steady ascent of 175ft (55m). We descend and head east, partly on a track and then along a lane before turning north along field paths to two small villages, Saunderton and Horsenden, both with moated sites and medieval churches. After Horsenden further field paths lead back to Bledlow. There are stretches along lanes and on roads in the villages, sheep in the fields south of Horsenden and ponies in the paddocks east of Bledlow.

The route gives some long views over the Vale of Aylesbury and follows the Upper Icknield Way, an ancient trackway, visiting three historic villages at the foot of the Chilterns.

MIDSOMER COMES TO BLEDLOW AND HORSENDEN

The walk starts near the Lions of Bledlow pub in, of course, Bledlow. The pub has seen several transformations for *Midsomer Murders*: as The Dog and Partridge in 'King's Crystal', The Feathers in 'A Rare Bird' and The Queen's Arms in 'Dead Man's 11'. It and the village have featured in other episodes, including 'Blue Herring', 'Dark Autumn', 'The House in the Woods' and 'A Worm in the Bud'. The fine parish church features as Badger's Drift's church in 'The Killings at Badger's Drift' and in 'Death's Shadow'. Horsenden's Gate Cottage featured in 'Ring Out Your Dead' as Maisie Grouch's house.

Much of the route is dog friendly but on the lanes, in the villages and in the sheep-grazed pastures they should be on leads.

No public toilets so rely on those in the pub, the Lions of Bledlow.

Park in Bledlow, near the Lions of Bledlow at the west end of the village.

There is only one pub actually on the route, the well-known Lions of Bledlow, which is popular with Ridgeway National Trail walkers as it's only a minor diversion from the national trail. It serves a good range of food and bar snacks.

The postcode for the Lions of Bledlow pub is HP27 9PE.

Ordnance Survey Explorer 181.

A BIT OF HISTORICAL BACKGROUND

There is an old rhyme about Bledlow: 'They that do live and do abide shall see the church fall in the Lyde.' This is a reference to the fine parish church which sits near the edge of The Lyde, a deep-cut 'coombe' from which springs emerge to feed the Lyde Brook, an inconsequential stream that heads north and used to power several watermills in the vale beyond. So far the church has remained standing and not tumbled into The Lyde, now a superbly landscaped garden that descends the hill with a number of ponds, designed by Robert Adam (the modern one) in 1967 for Lord and Lady Carrington.

Bledlow has Bledlow Manor at its east end, the Georgian mansion of Lord Carrington, and at the west end Manor Farm, a fascinating house of medieval and Tudor origins. In between is the parish church of Holy Trinity (in medieval times Holy Spirit), with its four-bay nave and aisles dating from about 1200, a fair amount of medieval wall painting traces and a superb Norman communion chalice-style font (a regional speciality known collectively as 'Aylesbury Fonts').

Horsenden's Gate Cottage featured in 'Ring Out Your Dead' as Maisie Grouch's house.

THE WALK

1. We parked near the Lions of Bledlow pub and bore left on to the track, signed 'Bridleway to the Ridgeway', past its car park and followed the path until it bore right. We continued ahead, the track climbing between hedges and trees. Reaching the Ridgeway National Trail we turned left on to it and followed the track to a road.

2. Continuing ahead, we walked along a quiet lane, here followed by the Icknield Way Trail. We crossed a road, Lee Road, passed beneath a railway bridge and, opposite the Old Rectory, turned left to leave the lane on to the Chiltern Way.

Stop, look and listen. A Chiltern Railways mainline train crosses the footpath near Horsendon as it speeds to Birmingham.

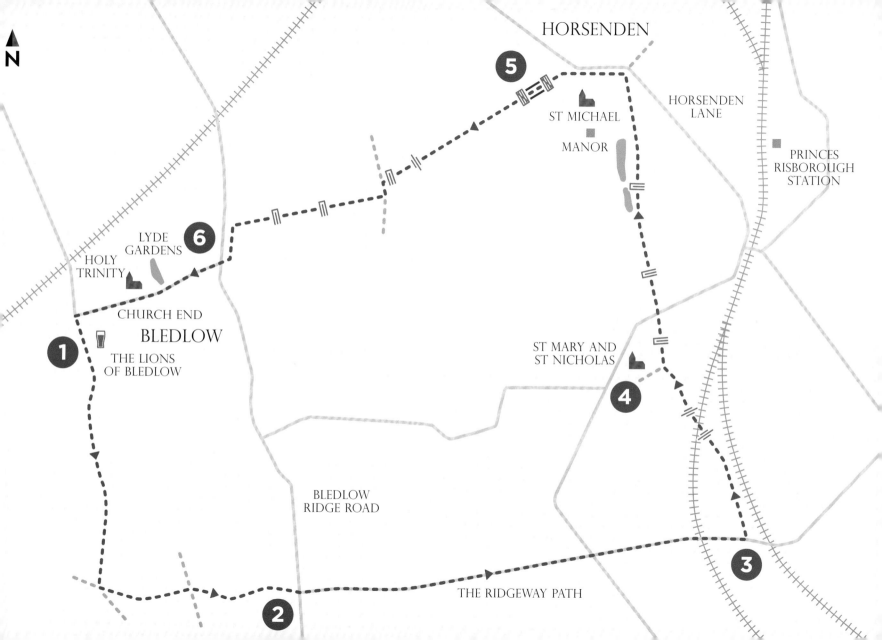

N

HORSENDEN

⑤

HORSENDEN
LANE

ST MICHAEL

MANOR

PRINCES
RISBOROUGH
STATION

LYDE
GARDENS

⑥

HOLY
TRINITY

CHURCH END

BLEDLOW

①

THE LIONS
OF BLEDLOW

ST MARY AND
ST NICHOLAS

④

BLEDLOW
RIDGE ROAD

③

②

THE RIDGEWAY PATH

3. Now in a pasture between two railway lines, initially we followed a grassy path alongside a garden, then alongside scrub around a spring-fed stream. We crossed the railway via a bridge, steps and a stile, noting two lengths of Brunel's broad-gauge track reused as a braced fence post. We descended the other side of the Chiltern Railways' down line to Birmingham and crossed a stile.

We left the railway, which was originally the Wycombe Railway that reached Princes Risborough in 1862, and then became part of the Great Central Railway that ran from Marylebone to Birmingham and the north, this stretch to Banbury opening in 1905. We walked along the field edge alongside a stream within the scrub to our left, going left at a footpath sign.

We walked beside a moated site, apparently part of a long-abandoned Norman motte and bailey castle, the moated bailey once improved and occupied by Saunderton's manor house: all gone and scrub and trees have taken over.

Trees near Horsenden.

The fine parish church features as Badger's Drift's church in 'The Killings at Badger's Drift' and in 'Death's Shadow'.

4. Through a kissing gate we visited the churchyard of St Mary and St Nicholas' parish church, its village also long gone with only one old cottage remaining plus a few houses, mostly modern. The churchyard is quiet and charming but the church, with its attractive bellcote, is rarely open.

We retraced our steps to the path alongside the field and bore left to reach a kissing gate. Through this we passed along a path, a garden fence on our right, and crossed the road on to the drive to Brook Cottage. We crossed a garden, skirting along its right edge following a permissive path or continue straight ahead – we did the decent, privacy-respecting thing and used the permissive path.

Out through a kissing gate we followed the field edge alongside a stream. Now in sheep pasture we felt ourselves truly in the Midlands, sheep grazing beneath parkland trees. Through another kissing gate we continued in more sheep pasture, the low December sun casting long shadows of trees and sheep. To our left we passed another moated site, then a series of medieval fishponds, enlarged to ornamental lakes for Horsenden House, but largely screened from public gaze. Out through another kissing gate we turned left on to the lane through Horsenden village.

On the left are the gates to Horsenden House and on the right the thatched cottage, Gate Cottage, which was used as Maisie Grouch's cottage in 'Ring Out Your Dead'.

Horsenden House, the old manor house, has a long and complex architectural history. From the lane it looks Georgian with Regency ends, but within is a Tudor house and even the Georgian front was rediscovered only a few years ago. It is the residence of Jason Kay of the Jamiroquai band fame and who has been an enthusiastic restorer of his house. Hence the 'Space Cowboy' reference in the walk title, one of his best-known hits. At the north-west corner of the manor house grounds is the parish church of St Michael in a pretty churchyard. It looks truncated and it is: the nave was pulled down in 1765 and the present west tower was built at the same time, only the fifteenth-century chancel remained to serve as the parish church, extended in the nineteenth century, presumably to accommodate more villagers. However, this is another church that is rarely open to the public.

5. Just past the church we went through a hand gate on to a path, passing to the right of the barns of Manor Farm. We crossed to a hand gate ahead and, over a footbridge, continued across an arable field, Bledlow's tree-covered The Cop ahead on the Chiltern escarpment. We carried on ahead on a grassy track alongside a hedge to a path T-junction. Over a stile we turned left, then soon turned right through a kissing gate into pasture to continue alongside a hedge, continuing through a kissing gate towards farm buildings. Through another kissing gate we followed a track past outbuildings with collections of old farm implements, ploughs and harrows.

6. At the road we turned left and followed it for some yards, taking care, as it can be busy. Reaching Bledlow village just before we turned right, we looked at the three ranges of the late eighteenth-century former workhouse on our left, currently undergoing a sluggish conversion to housing. We turned right into the village main street, Church End, with on our left the walls and grounds of Bledlow Manor, a fine eighteenth-century red-brick house. Before we reached the church we visited The Lyde Gardens, which were laid out around springs that feed into streams running north into the clay vale. We descended past ponds formed by damming the springs with a fine collection of damp-loving plants and some modern sculpture. Lord and Lady Carrington of Bledlow Manor laid out these gardens, originally for the use only of villagers, but now for the enjoyment of any visitors to Bledlow.

After visiting the church, which is often open, we refreshed ourselves at the Lions of Bledlow, a pub popular with Ridgeway walkers.

The Lions of Bledlow has seen several transformations for Midsomer Murders: *as The Dog and Partridge in 'King's Crystal', The Feathers in 'A Rare Bird' and The Queen's Arms in 'Dead Man's 11'.*

FIT FOR PRINCES AND SMUGGLERS 5.5 MILES (8.8KM)

Cadsden, Monks Risborough and Princes Risborough

INTRODUCTION

This walk combines the Chiltern Hills and the flat land of the Vale of Aylesbury, packing in a fine market town as well as smaller villages and hamlets in its 5.5 miles. Mostly it is on footpaths, tracks and woodland trails, but there is some road work in and out of Princes Risborough. There was little or no livestock alongside or on the route when we walked it.

The route involves a steep descent from the Chilterns, eased by timber steps, and a climb back up from Cadsden. It follows parts of the Ridgeway National Trail.

 Much of the route is dog friendly but in Princes Risborough, the hamlets and on the short stretches of road, dogs should be on leads.

 There are public toilets in Princes Risborough town centre.

 Park in the Whiteleaf Cross and Hill public car park off Peters Lane, at the highest point of the walk.

 The Plough at Cadsden (Point 9) is excellent and actually on the Ridgeway National Trail, while in Princes Risborough we passed two pubs, the George and Dragon and the Whiteleaf Cross, as well as several cafes, including La Crêpe Escape, Costa and Anton Hazells.

 The Whiteleaf Hill and Cross car park has the postcode HP27 0LL.

 Ordnance Survey Explorer 181.

MIDSOMER COMES TO PRINCES RISBOROUGH, MONKS RISBOROUGH AND CADSDEN

This walk takes in three locations used in *Midsomer Murders*, the first being in Princes Risborough itself where Wycombe District Council's former Princes Risborough Information Centre was converted into Causton Social Services for a scene in 'Shot at Dawn'. Inside, the plaque used in the filming is kept and it is hoped that it will soon be installed in the public area of the information centre as a tourist attraction. Later in the walk the thatched cottages in Burton Lane in nearby Monks Risborough featured in 'Ring Out Your Dead', as did the sound of St Dunstan's church bells in the same episode, although not the church itself. The third location used was The Plough at Cadsden where we had lunch. This was seen in 'Down Among the Dead Men'.

A BIT OF HISTORICAL BACKGROUND

Monks Risborough is a village with three rectories: a grand seventeenth-century one, a smaller 1920s one and an even smaller modern one in the latter's former garden. Although somewhat swamped by modern housing estates, Monks Risborough retains a village character, centred on Burton Lane and the Aylesbury Road. West of these are the oldest rectory and the very fine parish church of St Dunstan. A remnant of Place Farm survives as a public park, which provides a decent open setting for the farm's large sixteenth-century stone dovecote with a pyramid roof.

Monks Risborough got its name to distinguish it from Princes Risborough and was held by Christchurch Priory in Canterbury from the tenth century until Henry VIII's Dissolution of the Monasteries. This is probably why there is a tenth-century charter setting out the parish boundary, much of the landmarks still being traceable. The charter was probably a forgery or copy of a later one produced by the monks but remains interesting nonetheless.

Princes Risborough got its name from the Black Prince, appointed custodian of the manor of what had previously been called Great Risborough in 1343 by his father Edward III. It was already a royal stud farm and deer park by 1305 and provided the Black Prince's great warhorses as well as riding and hunting ones. The park was west of the town but is now built over, while the manor house, stud buildings and stables were on the site of the current Mount car park immediately next to the parish church. In short the historic cores of both Monks and Princes Risborough have been somewhat surrounded by modern development, but if you use your imagination you can get a feel for their pre-twentieth-century form.

THE WALK

1. We met at the Whiteleaf Cross and Hill public car park high in the Chiltern Hills at about 685ft above sea level (250m), hoping for superb long views across Princes Risborough and the Vale of Aylesbury far below. The sun had disappeared behind clouds and it was a chilly early March morning when we set off, although sunshine was promised for the early afternoon.

From the car park we crossed the road to a kissing gate, which led into Brush Hill Local Nature Reserve, a reserve with two parts, the first part wooded. We took the right-hand path through the wood to join the Ridgeway National Trail at a kissing gate. Through this gate we reached the open downland part of the reserve and headed for a flint-built viewpoint pillar. From here we enjoyed the long views with Bledlow Cop away to our left along the Chiltern escarpment and the vast expanse of the Vale of Aylesbury and far into Oxfordshire. We descended the grassy ridge to another kissing gate where the Ridgeway National Trail descends steeply off the

The Ridgeway path.

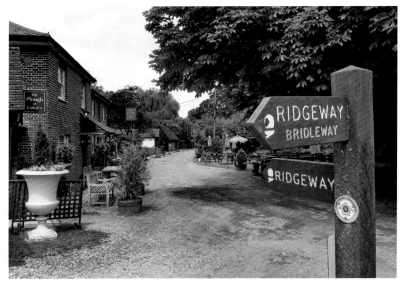

The Plough at Cadsden, seen in 'Down Among the Dead Men'.

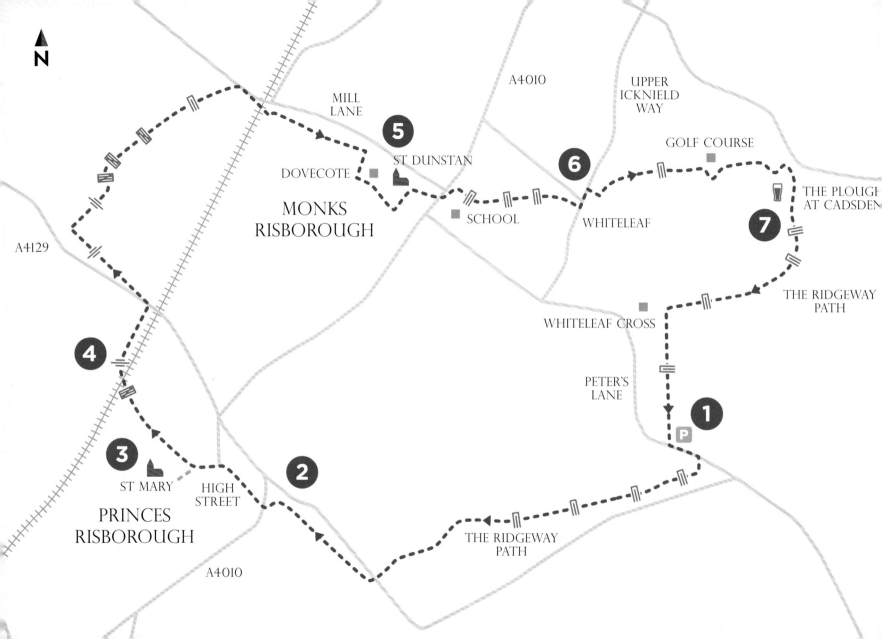

N

MILL LANE

5 ST DUNSTAN

DOVECOTE

MONKS RISBOROUGH

A4129

SCHOOL

A4010

UPPER ICKNIELD WAY

GOLF COURSE

6

WHITELEAF

THE PLOUGH AT CADSDEN

7

THE RIDGEWAY PATH

WHITELEAF CROSS

PETER'S LANE

4

3 ST MARY

PRINCES RISBOROUGH

HIGH STREET

2

A4010

1

P

THE RIDGEWAY PATH

Chilterns through woodland via a long flight of timber steps, renewed in 2013 by the Chiltern Society. At the bottom we left the woods to continue ahead along the Ridgeway National Trail beside a hedge and turned left to join a well-hedged track. Soon passing between gardens, we reached a road where we turned right to descend towards Princes Risborough, passing through a 1950s housing estate.

2.   At the roundabout there is a large pudding stone set in an area of Denner Hill setts. Both stones come from the Chilterns, the latter from a couple of miles north of High Wycombe, and are the product of the extreme pressure on local sandy and pebbly soils by the ice sheets that crushed most of England thousands of years ago. The name derives from a superficial similarity to a plum pudding and this one was found nearby in 1984 when the road was widened.

We crossed at the pelican crossing to look at the council's former Risborough Information Centre, which was transformed into Causton Social Services in the 'Shot at Dawn' episode. Past this we turned right into the High Street, which

Plaque on Amy Johnson's house in Princes Risborough.

Thatched cottages in Monks Risborough featured in 'Ring Out Your Dead'.

Neolithic mound, Whiteleaf.

seems to have more cafes than pubs, and at the Market House we went left into Church Street. More interesting brick and timber-framed houses lead to the parish church, which is normally open during the day. Beyond this is an unromantic car park, The Mount, which was once thought to be the site of the Black Prince's fourteenth-century palace. In fact, as the background section notes, it was more likely to have been a stud farm for his warhorses and hunters. Anyway you have to use your imagination to see it as it was in the Middle Ages.

3. Back through the churchyard, we turned left up the un-surfaced Church Lane, which passes the fine seventeenth-century brick facade of the manor house. On the left, the cottage with the tall stone chimney is Monks Staithe where Amy Johnson, the famous aviatrix, lived in the late 1930s. We followed the path alongside a small stream, housing on the right and a park on the left, to the railway line. This is the old Wycombe Railway branch from Princes Risborough to Aylesbury that opened in 1863. Mercifully it survived the Beeching cuts and still has regular services. Through a hand gate we climbed steps up the embankment to cross the line and descend again to a stile where we turned right on to the path that continued alongside the railway line. At the main road we crossed it and turned left to walk along the pavement as far as a stile.

4. Over the stile and in ridge and furrowed pasture we walked alongside a hedge to another stile and then skirted a garden to emerge at the east end of the small hamlet of Alscot. Here we turned right through a hand gate and continued east in pasture, alongside a fence then hedges to pass through two further hand gates to a final one to cross a stream and reach a road. We turned right and passed under the railway along Mill Lane, the whitewashed former mill house on our right.

The Pudding Stone, Princes Risborough.

Monks Risborough's St Dunstan church. The sound of its bells were heard in 'Ring Out Your Dead'.

Beyond Kings Oak Close we went right into a park to walk towards the sixteenth-century pyramid-roofed stone dovecote, noting the pollarded willow near it which is a survivor of Place Farm, now vanished under the 1960s housing estate. From here we headed for St Dunstan's church, usually open during the day.

5. From the church porch we headed for the churchyard gate to the left of the modern timber-clad church hall. At the T-junction we turned left to walk past the thatched cottages seen in 'Ring Out Your Dead'. At the junction we turned right and at the war memorial's Celtic-style cross, turned left along the main road, the A4010, to cross at a pelican crossing in front of the Victorian brick and flint primary school, immediately bearing right at a hand gate on to a path to skirt the playground. At a kissing gate we bore half left across pasture to another kissing gate to pass between gardens to a further kissing gate. Here we turned right on to a lane and at the junction we entered the hamlet of Whiteleaf.

6. We turned briefly left on to the Upper Icknield Way and then right at the footpath sign, the Icknield Way Riders Route, before going left on to a drive, soon reaching a footpath between garden fences. This path emerged on to the access drive to the Whiteleaf Golf Club, where we turned right and, at a waymark, left to cross the cricket ground to a hand gate to the left of the pavilion. Through this we crossed the golf fairway, checking that no players were driving off the tee to our left, and crossed to a cottage. The path skirts to its right, then left along its east side. Next the path bore right and we followed it over a ridge, the golf course beyond a tree belt on the right. The path then descended into the hamlet of Lower Cadsden: a few cottages, a farmstead and the pub.

7. The Plough at Cadsden is, famously, the only pub on the whole of the Ridgeway National Trail and featured in the 'Down Among the Dead Men' episode. It does a brisk trade with walkers and locals and was a welcome refreshment break for us before we climbed back towards Whiteleaf Hill.

Suitably refreshed and now on the Ridgeway National Trail, we turned right by the pub's gated car park and very shortly took the left fork, passing through a kissing gate and forking right to ascend steadily, staying on the Ridgeway National Trail at a cross path.

The path climbs through beech woods, with some old giants fallen over in the very wet winter of 2013–14, to a kissing gate that leads to the open grassland of Whiteleaf Hill with a Neolithic barrow mound to our left and fine views across the Vale of Aylesbury but a less satisfactory view of the top of the Whiteleaf Cross. This is obviously best seen from afar in the vale part of this walk.

We turned left to a hand gate beside a field gate and continued along the Ridgeway National Trail along the top of the ridge, bearing left off it to return to the car park and the end of the walk.

The Plough at Cadsden seen in 'Down Among the Dead Men'.

Princes Risborough Information Centre, which was Causton Social Services centre in 'Shot at Dawn'.

WALK 8 ROUTE AND BRANCH LINES 5.5 MILES (8.8KM)

Watlington

INTRODUCTION

This is a pretty straightforward walk, mostly on tracks and quiet lanes with some footpaths as well as pavements in Watlington itself. The footpaths can be muddy in winter but there were no livestock alongside or on the route when we walked it, apart from dog walkers.

The route avoids a steep climb into the Chilterns, the Ridgeway National Trail skirting its foot along the ancient route of the Icknield Way.

Watlington undercroft market.

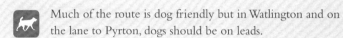 Much of the route is dog friendly but in Watlington and on the lane to Pyrton, dogs should be on leads.

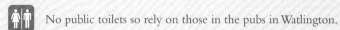 No public toilets so rely on those in the pubs in Watlington.

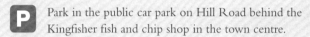 Park in the public car park on Hill Road behind the Kingfisher fish and chip shop in the town centre.

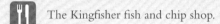 The Kingfisher fish and chip shop.

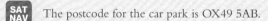 The postcode for the car park is OX49 5AB.

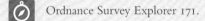 Ordnance Survey Explorer 171.

MIDSOMER COMES TO WATLINGTON

Watlington has proved popular with *Midsomer Murders* location finders and our route through this small market town passes several sites, apart from the rather disappointing parish church, which featured in 'Ring Out Your Dead'. The red-brick Town Hall, prominently located in the centre of the town and dating from the 1660s, had an unusual dual function then as a boys' grammar school upstairs and market hall below. It appeared in 'Judgement Day', as did Calnan's butchers shop (Ray Dorset's in the episode) in the High Street. At the west end of the High Street, opposite the war memorial cross, Griffith's estate agents served as

'Beauvoisin Estates' in 'Dead Man's 11' and its interior was used for 'Midsomer Travel' in 'Orchis Fatalis'. The library became 'Causton Library', also in 'Orchis Fatalis', while the weatherboarded granary raised on its staddle stones became 'Harvey Crane's Antiques' shop in 'Midsomer Rhapsody'. Most spectacularly, Church Street was turned into a neglected and shabby Lower Warden for 'A Tale of Two Hamlets' and in Chapel Street the thatched No. 42 featured as the 'Ellis Bell' museum in that episode.

A BIT OF HISTORICAL BACKGROUND

Watlington originally grew up near the parish church at the north-west end of the town where there was a royal manor house, probably built for Richard of Cornwall, brother of Henry III who became King of the Romans in 1257 as well as Earl of Cornwall. His principal local seat was Wallingford Castle not far away and he also had a hunting park at Watlington for the relaxations of the chase, now where Watlington Park is on the Chiltern slopes south-east of the town. In the fourteenth century a royal licence to crenellate, that is erect battlements, was granted for the manor house to a successor. By the seventeenth century, however, it had been demolished and the stone and timber reused in houses in the town. Near the church there was also a monastic grange or farm owned and run by the monks of Oseney Abbey near Oxford. By the fifteenth century the centre of gravity of the town had shifted to the Shirburn Street/Couching Street/High Street area and the church is now in something of a backwater.

There was much coming and going of Royalist and Parliamentarian troops in the area during the English Civil War, with Royalist troops stationed in the town in 1642 and stripping the area of hay for their horses, wheat, bread and anything else they could get their hands on in an era when an army lived off the land rather than from its supply trains. Watlington was between Aylesbury, which was stoutly Parliamentarian, and Oxford where King Charles I had his headquarters, so skirmishes were frequent. At other times the Parliamentarian forces occupied the town and stripped the surrounding countryside of hay, fodder and provisions in their turn.

In 1665 Thomas Stonor of Stonor Park and the then lord of the manor, paid for the Town Hall and founded the grammar school, apparently in gratitude for the Restoration of King Charles II. The town still has many good buildings, ranging

Watlington Town Hall appeared in 'Judgement Day', as did Calnan's butchers shop (Ray Dorset's in this episode) in the High Street.

from cruck houses and timber-framed and thatched ones to superior Georgian ones. It retains a distinct small-town character with a surprising number of minor shops that are not part of national concerns.

The route passes the erstwhile terminus of the Watlington and Princes Risborough Railway (Point 5), next to Pyrton Field Farm. Thus the railway terminated half a mile from the town it purported to serve. The reason for this was because this was where the Earl of Macclesfield's land ended and the adjoining landowner could not be persuaded to join the other investors. The earl, based at nearby Shirburn Castle, was one of the main promoters and investors in the railway authorised by an Act of Parliament in 1859, finally opening in 1872. Never a success, it was a 'light railway' with inferior trackwork laid directly on the chalk without ballast. No wonder the Great Western Railway was reluctant to take it over and when it was finally persuaded to do so they had to lay the whole line again and build anew the stations and infrastructure. They paid £23,000 for it, half the cost the investors had put into the substandard original.

THE WALK

1. We met in the free public car park in the centre of Watlington in Hill Road and behind the Kingfisher fish and chip shop. Fortunately it was a sunny morning, the days either side having been very rainy and unpleasant. We left the car park past an old red telephone kiosk, Giles Gilbert Scott's 1935 well-known K6 'Jubilee' design. At the village crossroads we turned left by the fish and chip shop to head down Couching Street, the seventeenth-century red-brick Town Hall on our right. Halfway down on the left, No. 20 has a bulbous old shop window and above it nineteenth-century painted lettering reads 'Tallow {Kitchen} Chandler': a rare survival. At the end of the road is a fine timber-framed house, The Lilacs, which closes the vista down Couching Street. Here we turned right on to Brook Street, soon leaving it at a left turn on to a footpath by an electricity pole.

Watlington Town Hall appeared in 'Judgement Day'.

The estate agents served as Beauvoisin Estates in 'Dead Man's 11' and its interior was used for Midsomer Travel in 'Orchis Fatalis'.

2. We walked along the footpath beside a brick and limestone wall that became a chalk stone wall, the path pretty muddy on this January day. We passed through a kissing gate to cross a pasture diagonally to another kissing gate, this field much used by local dog walkers. We bore left alongside a stream, again accompanied by mud. Reaching a metalled track we bore left along it. At a string of ponds maintained as a nature reserve by the farmer the metalled track becomes a path alongside them.

Beyond the ponds we continued along the hedgeless track between huge arable fields as far as an ivy-covered hedge where the path bears right, then left alongside a concrete farm access road, a hedge and fence between it and us. Over a stile and our path met the Ridgeway National Trail, here following the ancient Icknield Way.

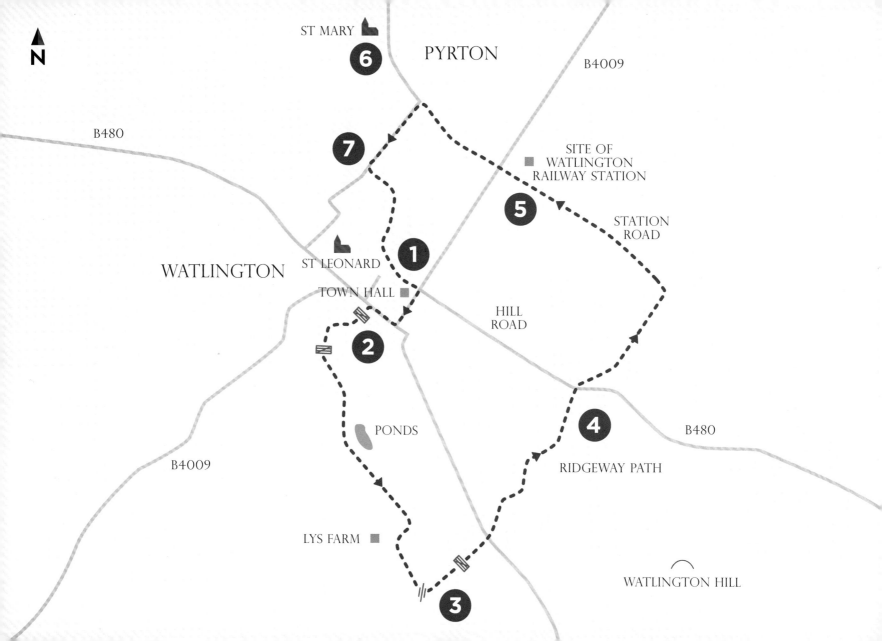

N

PYRTON

ST MARY

6

B4009

B480

7

SITE OF
WATLINGTON
RAILWAY STATION

5

STATION
ROAD

WATLINGTON

ST LEONARD

1

TOWN HALL

HILL
ROAD

2

PONDS

4

B480

B4009

RIDGEWAY PATH

LYS FARM

WATLINGTON HILL

3

3. However, instead of going left along the concrete farm road that is the Ridgeway here, the farmer has provided a permissive path on the opposite side, complete with a bench for the weary traveller. We followed the permissive path, which rejoins the Ridgeway National Trail via a gate just before it crosses the B480 road. We crossed the road and continued past Icknield House along the Ridgeway with early snowdrops in places alongside the path.

The weatherboarded granary raised on its staddle stones.

The Granary became Harvey Crane's antiques shop in 'Midsomer Rhapsody'.

4. The next road is Hill Road, which leads to Christmas Common and Watlington Hill where a house was used in 'The Killings at Badger's Drift' and in 'Ring Out Your Dead'. Across this we continued alongside woods at the foot of the hill, wood smoke drifting across from clearance work in the nature reserve. Past the conifer plantation we crossed the old boundary between Watlington and Pyrton parishes. Reaching a junction with a lane we turned left on to it, this being the old track that linked Pyrton village to its hill pasture on Pyrton Hill behind us.

5. Beyond Pyrton Park Farm is the site of Watlington Station where what looks like a narrow, corrugated-iron-clad Dutch barn is in fact the railway's carriage shed while the station building can be discerned in deep decay amid ivy and scrub. The line opened in 1872 and ran to Princes Risborough but closed in 1960 and features in several of these walks (Walks 9 and 20) but it is noteworthy that it terminated in Pyrton parish, the Watlington parish boundary on the opposite side of the lane and half a mile from the town.

We continued to the crossroads with the B4009 and crossed to head towards Pyrton, the holm oaks lining the road on the right marking the boundary of Shirburn Park, still following the Oxfordshire Way path. In the centre of this park is Shirburn Castle, which received its licence to crenellate in 1377 and was unusually built in brick. The castle was heavily altered by the earls of Macclesfield in the eighteenth and nineteenth centuries, but cannot be seen from our route. At a T-junction we continued ahead, passing one of the Shirburn gate lodges, now called the Lodge House, a mid-Victorian building, to walk into Pyrton village.

6. Reaching this attractive small village we visited its parish church. It was largely rebuilt in the nineteenth century but reused older elements such as the Norman south doorway and its Jacobean pulpit. The village is worth exploring with some very fine houses, including the Jacobean manor house and two vicarages, the eighteenth-century one replacing the seventeenth-century one.

Watlington Library became Causton Library in 'Orchis Fatalis'.

Watlington's little market.

We retraced our steps to the Shirburn gate lodge and turned right along the lane towards Watlington. At the school playing field fence we turned left on to a footpath that skirts the playing field, an arable field on our left. The path bore right with allotments to our left and became a lane, passing the gates to the school, Icknield Community College. We continued across Paul's Way and passed The Chequers pub into Chapel Street. We continued on Chapel Street as it bore left towards the town centre, ignoring New Road.

7. At the war memorial we turned left to walk along the High Street with its fine mix of timber-framed buildings and Georgian houses, passing Griffith and Partners, the library (Causton Library) and The Granary which all featured in *Midsomer Murders*. Back at the Town Hall, which featured in 'Judgement Day', we crossed the road and again passed the fish and chip shop to return to the car park.

A bench for the weary.

WALK 9 VANISHED RAILWAYS AND LEATHERN BOTTLES 5.5 MILES (8.8KM)

Lewknor

INTRODUCTION

This attractive walk at the foot of the Chiltern escarpment has few navigational difficulties and its two villages (Lewknor and Aston Rowant) are delightful, both with very interesting parish churches. Apart from the two villages, the route is on footpaths and tracks. There was no livestock alongside or on the route when we walked it: except for horses being exercised from the Aston Rowant Stud, and, of course, dogs being walked.

The route follows a stretch of the Ridgeway National Trail skirting the foot of Beacon Hill along the ancient route of the Upper Icknield Way.

The route is dog friendly but in the two villages and when crossing roads dogs should be on leads.

No public toilets so rely on those in The Leathern Bottle pub in Lewknor.

Park on the village roads in Lewknor.

The Leathern Bottle in Lewknor does excellent food and welcomes well-behaved dogs.

SAT NAV High Street, Lewknor, OX49 5TW.

Ordnance Survey Explorer 171.

MIDSOMER COMES TO LEWKNOR AND ASTON ROWANT

Lewknor village sits on a dead-end High Street, severed by the M40 after it cuts through the Chilterns to cross the clay vales of Oxfordshire. The B4009 bypassed the village and this road is now an official car park for those catching coaches to London or car sharing. Unfortunately this has proved inadequate so commuters are now cluttering the village itself. However, the village retains its charm, as does Aston Rowant, also set on a dead end. This walk focuses on the spring line where the villages grew up and also skirts, on the Ridgeway National Trail, the foot of the Chiltern escarpment in the lee of Beacon Hill.

For *Midsomer Murders* fans, Lewknor appeared in several episodes: a cottage in Church Road became Megan's House in 'Death and Dust' while the parish church exterior featured in 'A Tale of Two Hamlets', as did the school in this episode, and in 'The House in the Woods'.

Aston Rowant had three locations, all seen on the walk route: the Fluxes House, a thatched cottage made from flint and brick which appears in 'The House in the Woods', and two sites at the east end of the village green. These last two stand side by side and both appear in 'A Sacred Trust', the left-hand building as The Vertue Arms and the adjacent whitewashed one with two bay windows as Midsomer Vertue's village stores.

A BIT OF HISTORICAL BACKGROUND

Lewknor and Aston Rowant are villages on the spring line where water appears from beneath the chalk, each side of the old London to Oxford coach road, now the A40. They were also between much more ancient routes which ran south-west to north-east, the Upper and Lower Icknield Ways, the lower a summer route and converted to a Roman road. Now, of course, the Chilterns are rudely cut through by the M40, which passes uncomfortably close to Lewknor. Further south the Watlington branch railway line (1872–1960) had a station and goods yard to serve Aston Rowant and a halt for Lewknor, the former near the Ridgeway National Trail but demolished and overgrown while Lewknor's halt disappeared under the M40 and the diversion of the B4009: quite a long and full transport history for the two villages.

The chief glories of both villages are their parish churches, Lewknor's with fine monuments, the biggest in the north transept's Jodrell family chapel. In the chancel are two fine seventeenth-century alabaster pairs of effigies and there is a modest wall plaque to Sir Paul Getty of Wormsley Park in Stokenchurch who died in 2003. The Norman font has a primitive power with rows of beaded interlocking circles, but the finest work is in the chancel with richly ornate sedilia (seat recesses) and piscine complete with ribbed vaulting – an impressive church where wealthy patrons were happy to spend money on its enrichment. Aston Rowant's church is simpler but equally rewarding, with a fair amount

of fourteenth and fifteenth-century stained glass, a range of fine monuments, an ornate Purbeck marble thirteenth-century font and two triple-arched tomb recesses. The list could go on but we should mention the 'squint' cut through the north chapel wall to give the priest at the Lady Chapel altar sight of the main altar so the priests could raise the Host (the consecrated bread) at the same moment during the Mass.

For railway buffs the stretch of the Watlington branch offers Great Western Railway fences and a chance to reminisce about the lost branch lines of England. Indeed several of the walks take in this branch, including its surviving track from Princes Risborough to Chinnor (Walks 6, 8, 9 and 20).

THE WALK

1. We set off from Lewknor on a mixed sunny and cloudy October day, having looked at the 1836 school, a curious building with the schoolmaster's house looking like a small hipped-roof, early nineteenth-century farmhouse flanked by thatched schoolrooms and which featured in *Midsomer Murders* episodes. We walked through the churchyard lychgate with its mossy roof and fortunately the church was open. You never know how good an interior can be, even if you've read about it, and St Margaret's church is full of treasures: a Norman font, superb alabaster and stone monuments, and a lavish chancel rebuilt in the fourteenth century.

Leaving the church we set off in the sunshine, white cotton wool clouds racing across the sky, and joined the path between the church and the school via a gate at the churchyard's north-east corner (behind the chancel). Through a metal kissing gate we continued ahead on a grassy path on the margin of a large arable field, the roar of the M40 to our right. The path winds along beside a stream and then bore right across part of the field towards the M40 embankment, then left alongside it. We passed a stile into the edge of a copse, then bore right to pass beneath the motorway and continued ahead, the path now in a tree belt.

Aston Rowant Stud. Will the bird win?

2. Reaching the road, the A40, we turned left on to it, opposite the Blue Cross's Lewknor Rehoming Centre, which finds new homes for dogs and cats. We turned right on to a 'Restricted Byway', a lane that becomes a grassy track where you may meet volunteer dog walkers taking Blue Cross dogs for their constitutionals.

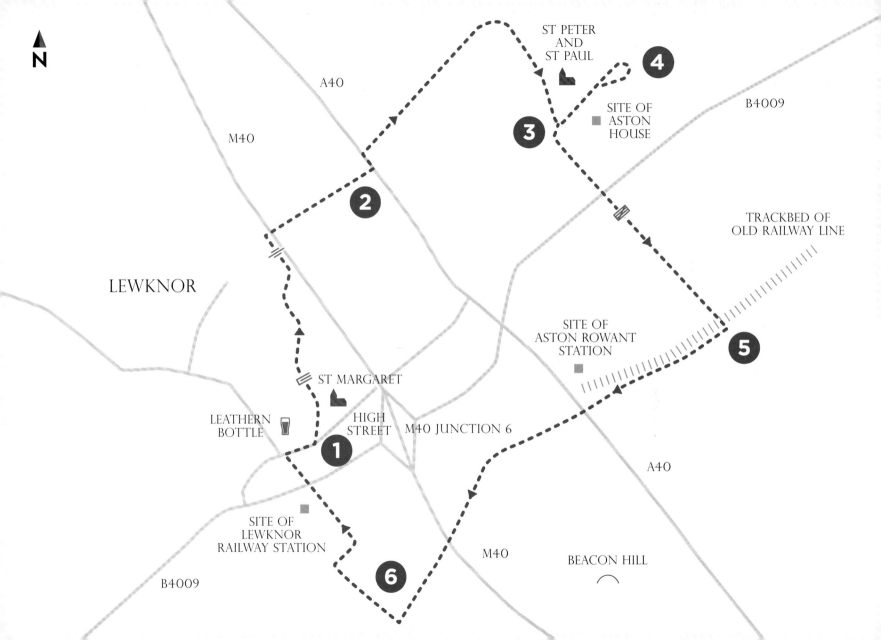

N

A40

M40

LEWKNOR

ST PETER
AND
ST PAUL

4

SITE OF
ASTON
HOUSE

B4009

3

TRACKBED OF
OLD RAILWAY LINE

2

SITE OF
ASTON ROWANT
STATION

5

ST MARGARET

LEATHERN
BOTTLE

HIGH
STREET

M40 JUNCTION 6

A40

1

SITE OF
LEWKNOR
RAILWAY STATION

M40

BEACON HILL

6

B4009

Autumn colours.

Aston Rowant Cottages.

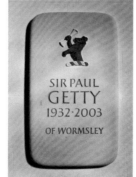

SIR PAUL
GETTY
1932·2003
OF WORMSLEY

Paul Getty, the American oil mogul, remembered in Lewknor church. His estate at Wormsley was close to Lewknor.

This path follows the route of the old Lower Icknield Way with hedges along some stretches on both or one side: a green lane. At the end we followed the lane right on to a metalled track and, at a five-way path junction we bore quarter right on to the route signed 'Aston Rowant'. The footpath soon enters a tree belt parallel to the lane, emerging on a track that turns into a lane into Aston Rowant. After a modern house we passed The Thatch, a flint cottage with white painted brick dressings that featured in 'The House in the Woods', before reaching the parish church.

3. Saints Peter and Paul parish church is situated at a T-junction in a grassy and well-treed churchyard and is another excellent church, usually open during the day, with a good collection of memorials and some medieval stained glass. From here we turned left along the lane to the village green, passing on the right the mid-nineteenth-century former stables, coach houses and service blocks to Aston House, then the set back gates to the noted Aston Rowant Stud. Just before the green and on our left is a Victorian model farmyard of 1867, now converted into dwellings.

4. On the far or east side of the green are two houses, side by side, that featured in *Midsomer Murders*: the left-hand flint and brick one became The Vertue Arms and the right-hand whitewashed one with two bay windows the Midsomer Vertue village store, both in 'A Sacred Trust'. We retraced our steps back past the church and continued ahead along the lane that curves left alongside a brick wall. This gave way to fences then passed the entrance to Aston Park. This was originally the drive to Aston House, which was gutted by fire in 1957. Now the grounds contain a number of modern houses but we could see evidence of the Victorian and Georgian parkland in the distance, the park lake still survives along with wellingtonias, cedars, limes and other parkland trees.

We continued along the lane to the main road, the B4009, and crossed to a bridle gate to follow the bridleway track south between arable fields. Horses from the Aston Rowant Stud often exercise in these fields and there are gallops in other fields. Several horses were being put through their paces when we walked the paths and the thunder of their hooves accompanied us as he headed along the track.

5. We passed through what seemed like a tree and scrub belt to turn right on to the Ridgeway National Trail. This belt is actually the course of the railway line that ran from Princes Risborough junction to Watlington (see Walk 8). The metal fence posts give a clue: they are old Great Western Railway broad-gauge rails bent into shape: waste not, want not, while the post and wire fences on either side of the old overgrown trackbed are classic Great Western also. The line opened in 1872 and closed in 1960.

We walked down the Ridgeway alongside the trackbed until it veered away from us to the site of Aston Rowant Station, which can be accessed by road from the A40. Reaching this road we crossed to continue along the Ridgeway National Trail, here a green lane with Beacon Hill rising up on our left. We passed an entrance to the Aston Rowant National Nature Reserve, which covers much of the hill and the fields on the south side of the path, and passed beneath the M40. Beyond we continued across a lane, Hill Farm Lane, to a footpath sign.

6. At this footpath sign we bore right to continue alongside a hedge, then went right to keep the reservoir on our left. At a lane we turned left and descended past the reservoir back to the A4009. Across the road we descended to join the lane into Lewknor and the end of the walk.

Exercising horses at Aston Rowant Stud.

Red Kites and The Vicar of Dibley

STONOR, TURVILLE, FINGEST, IBSTONE, WORMSLEY AND NETTLEBED

WALK 10 CATHOLIC REALM 3.5 MILES (5.7KM)

Stonor Park

INTRODUCTION

Stonor Park is a staggeringly beautifully located mellow brick-fronted country house with a long history. It is set on the north side of a wonderful valley, its walled gardens leading up towards a wooded ridge. The valley is an eastern spur from the one heading southwards to the Assendons and Henley: yet another picturesque Chiltern valley. Stonor Park house sits amid its deer park surrounded on three sides by woodland, the eastern sections much colonised by rhododendrons. With luck you should see the park's herds of fallow deer roaming and after the walk, if on a day when the house is open, the afternoon tea is jolly good.

After walking through Stonor village the path climbs out of the valley, then along a quiet lane before heading across fields to Southend. The route then turns west and is entirely within Stonor Park, the first third wooded, the rest open parkland with fine views of Stonor Park house in its valley. It is a delightful walk, packing in a good deal of excellent scenery in its relatively short length. The route is dog friendly but you may find cattle in fields near Southend.

MIDSOMER COMES TO STONOR

In the heart of the village the former Stonor Arms, now The Quince Tree after spectacular refurbishment and extension, was used in several episodes including 'Bad Tidings', 'Death and the Divas', 'A Worm in the Bud' and 'Death and Dreams', and Mungo Mortimer stayed here in 'Blue Herrings'. The cricket ground a little further north with the distinctive Round Clump copse behind it and opposite

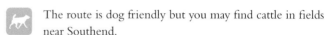 The route is dog friendly but you may find cattle in fields near Southend.

 No public toilets so rely on those in the pub en route.

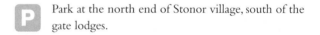 Park at the north end of Stonor village, south of the gate lodges.

The Quince Tree in Stonor village is a pub/restaurant and has a food shop as well. If you prefer a more village-y pub then keep going ahead for the Rainbow Inn in Middle Assendon, a mile or so south of Stonor.

The postcode of The Quince Tree in Stonor is RG9 6HE.

Ordnance Survey Explorer 171

the lodges and gates to Stonor Park featured in several episodes, as did Whitepond Farm at the road junction beyond the lodges. This farmhouse was seen in 'Bad Tidings', 'A Worm in the Bud', 'Electric Vendetta', and as Simon Bartlett's farm in 'Death and the Diva'.

We are not aware of Stonor Park house itself featuring specifically but the parkland is seen in some episodes.

A BIT OF HISTORICAL BACKGROUND

Stonor Park house has been held by the same family for over nine centuries. This impressive achievement is amplified by the fact that the family remained staunchly Roman Catholic throughout the long centuries after the Reformation. The house sits in a magnificent setting within a deer park and its oldest parts probably date from soon after 1280 when Sir Richard Stonor married Margaret Hornhull. The chapel was rebuilt about 1349 and there were numerous changes, including the early use of brick in the Chilterns in 1416. It is a complex house and the view of it from the route is of broadly symmetrical brick of the mid-eighteenth century, however this facade and side wings conceal a good deal of earlier work: medieval and Tudor. In the nineteenth century the Stonors were ennobled, taking the title of Lord Camoys, which they still hold. The house, the family and the deer park are a remarkable direct link with the thirteenth

Stonor footpath.

Stonor Park house.

century. It is difficult to think of a better setting for many miles in any direction and this route gives fine views of the house and its walled gardens as it runs along the southern side of the park's dry valley.

For once on these walks there are no parish churches as Stonor was, remarkably, part of Pyrton parish, a parish centred on that now small village, a virtual satellite of Watlington (Walk 8), while the other settlement on this walk, Southend, was a churchless hamlet in the parish of Turville (Walk 11). Southend's chief characteristic is a few cottages on the east side of a common pockmarked with old clay pits, some amid trees and flooded as ponds, that served the brick and tile kilns of the area: Kiln Cottage whose gates the route passes was the site of one of these kilns.

THE WALK

1. From the lay-bys north of the main village street we set off south to walk through the village, passing the Maidensgrove turn and The Quince Tree pub. The day was a sunny June one with the light intense, the clouds white and fluffy against a deep blue sky: perfect walking weather. There were several Stonor estate cottages with their distinctive, small-paned metal windows and rusticated quoins and window arches.

2. We passed the mainly seventeenth-century aisled barns of Upper Assendon Farm, extraordinarily still in agricultural use with cattle kept in the yards, and went left at the footpath sign over a stile and crossed pasture to another stile. Over this we were in woodland and climbing with yew trees alongside on our left. Where the path merged with a track we continued ahead and at a path junction continued ahead, a field to our left, soon passing to the left of a house, then to the right of barns to a kissing gate. Through this we went left along an access track to meet a lane.

County boundary. Oxfordshire on the right, Buckinghamshire on the left.

Stonor cricket ground and pavilion, used in several episodes.

3. At the lane we bore left and followed it, eventually bearing right. This quiet lane nips between Oxfordshire and Buckinghamshire and gives fine views south, seemingly for ever, or at least well into Berkshire. Reaching a T-junction we continued ahead, the signpost stating 'Henley 5'. We passed the gates to Kimble House and, reaching a footpath sign, bore left towards Kimble Farm between its gateposts. We followed the hedged drive and, at the sign for a permissive path, bore right alongside a post and rail fence. It is courteous to follow this permissive path as it avoids passing through the grounds of Kimble Farm. After some time the path descended and merged with the track that the statutory path followed through the farm.

Soon we reached a footpath sign at a crossways and bore left to climb within the edge of a wood. Reaching a stile we crossed it and, now on the Shakespeare Way waymarked path, continued ahead alongside a hedge and post and wire fence. On the day we walked the route there were handsome cattle in the field but well

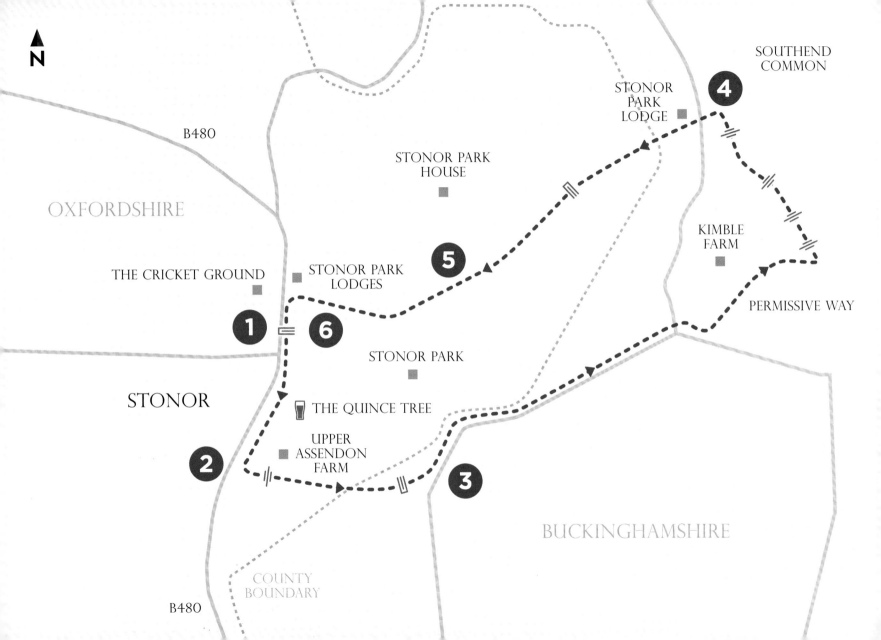

away to our right. We passed through the hedge via a stile and continued roughly alongside the hedge as it curved past a pond. Many of the ponds hereabouts are, not surprisingly, flooded former clay pits associated with a substantial now long-demolished brick kiln nearby. Reaching a stile we went over it, and then left alongside the hedge to another stile beside a gate.

4. Over this we were in Southend and on the track that passed the entrance to the evocatively named Kiln Cottage. Now on Southend Common, flooded clay pits were all around us. The great crested newt can, apparently, be found in these ponds. The track curved leftwards to the road, which we crossed on to a track that passes Nos 41 and 42 Southend. These are, in fact, outliers of the Stonor estate and architecturally are to the same design as many estate cottages in Stonor village itself. These mid-nineteenth-century estate cottages are quite elaborate with ornate wooden bargeboards and rusticated quoins and window arches.

We passed a field gate and entered the Stonor estate, descending along the track that is followed by both the Chiltern Way and by the Shakespeare Way on its way from the Globe Theatre to Stratford upon Avon. The woods, with their many tall pines and firs, are dense with rhododendrons, mostly the invasive ponticum, and in June very pretty with their pinkish purple flowers. The route is clear with waymark arrows on the trees and becomes a path descending through the woodland. We reached a tall kissing gate within the deer fence and continued descending, the path opening up and shortly heading across the grass and amid the parkland trees of the deer park.

5. The path follows the south side of the valley, well up the slopes, so the views of Stonor Park house are revealed gradually with its chapel and the walled gardens rising beyond. This stretch of the route is quite magical and over in the distance we saw a herd of the park's deer. There were also fine long views across the delightful rolling Chiltern landscape, funnelled by the valley to Pishill and beyond, the valley bearing left beyond Stonor village.

6. We reached the tall kissing gate out of the park and south of the Stonor lodges that flank the entrance to the main drive and, somewhat reluctantly on such a superbly sunny day, left the park and turned left to finish the walk.

Stonor Park.

WALK 11 DIBLEY IN THE VALLEY 4 MILES (6.4KM)

Turville and Fingest

INTRODUCTION

Turville has long been known for its use in films and TV series: indeed its alternative name these days is Dibley, St Mary's church serving as Dawn French's church in *The Vicar of Dibley*. You can see why as it's a delightful and quintessentially English village, nestling in a valley of the Chilterns. Up above the village, on the ridge to the north, is Cobstone Windmill, which featured in *Chitty Chitty Bang Bang* as the splendidly named Caractacus Potts' house. Besides this there are two superb Chiltern parish churches and beautiful scenery: the Hambleden Valley and its surrounding well-wooded hills.

The route climbs out of Turville to Cobstone Windmill, then curves to Fingest village, back in the valley, before climbing into the hills and descending to Skirmett, all on paths. From Skirmett the paths head west, then north back to Turville and a well-deserved pint and lunch in the Bull and Butcher.

MIDSOMER COMES TO TURVILLE AND FINGEST

Turville has featured in numerous episodes with the Bull and Butcher pub renamed 'The Spotted Cow' in 'Schooled in Murder'. It was also used in 'Murder on St Malley's Day' and other scenes for this episode were shot in the village as well as for 'The Straw Woman'. For the latter various village houses are seen while St Mary's church featured in a grisly way with characters burned alive inside it. The former village school, now a nursery, was used as the village hall. Various cottages and Cobstone Windmill were used in 'Murder on St Malley's Day' and the mill was also seen in 'Dark Autumn'.

The next village on the route, Fingest, had The Chequers Inn disguised as an antique shop in 'Country Matters' and it and The Old Rectory in Chequers Lane, opposite the churchyard, appeared in 'The Silent Land'.

 The route is dog friendly but you may find sheep in the fields east of Fingest.

 No public toilets so rely on those in the pubs en route.

 Park by the small village green in Turville.

 The Bull and Butcher in Turville is friendly, very well known and allows dogs in one of the bars. In Fingest there is The Chequers Inn and The Frog at Skirmett, its name a play on Kermit the Frog from *The Muppets*. All do good food, but we prefer the Bull and Butcher.

 The postcode for the Bull and Butcher in Turville village is RG9 6QU.

 Ordnance Survey Explorer 171.

A BIT OF HISTORICAL BACKGROUND

St Mary's church, Turville, set in a picturesque churchyard approached past sixteenth and seventeenth-century timber-framed cottages with mellow old tiled roofs is, of course, used as *The Vicar of Dibley*'s church but is well worth visiting in its own right. For us the best feature is the beautiful John Piper stained-glass lunette above the north door. It depicts a white hand holding a white lily

Fingest church.

Cobstone Windmill, used in 'Murder on St Malley's Day', was also seen in 'Dark Autumn'.

Hambleden Brook valley, Turville.

set in intense Bluebell-blue glass with an inscription, 'My soul doth magnify the Lord …' The glass was made by the equally celebrated stained-glass maker Patrick Reyntiens in 1975. One of Britain's finest painters and stained-glass artists, Piper lived at Fawley Bottom, at the far end of the Buckinghamshire Chilterns and not far from Henley, where he died in 1992.

There is much of interest in this delightful and intimately scaled medieval church with its squat square battlemented tower little higher than the nave roof ridge. The nave is basically Norman and the north chapel was built for the Perry family, the then lords of the manor, in 1733; their urn-topped marble monument dominates the chapel.

Skirmett is an oddly foreign-sounding name for a Chilterns village and is one of few Danish names found in this part of England. 'Skir' is a Danish version of the Old English 'shire' and 'mett' a version of 'mote' or meeting place so at some stage around AD 900 the Chiltern shire mote met in this part of the Hambleden valley. In the fourteenth century the name of the village is recorded as 'La Skiremote'. The shire meeting place itself is unknown but the other two villages on this route also have names of Danish origin: Tovi's vill or Turville and Fingest, originally Tinghurst, which is another assembly place, 'ting' continuing in Scandinavian use as 'Thing' or parliament 'storthing' (great assembly): a clutch of Danish settlers amid the Chiltern Anglo-Saxons.

Cobstone Mill.

THE WALK

1. We set off from Turville's small village green, having visited the parish church, on a drizzly early June day to head towards the windmill on the ridge overlooking the village, following a footpath along a gravel track between houses. Through a hand gate we continued ahead to a kissing gate and then climbed steeply towards the *Chitty Chitty Bang Bang* windmill where Roy Boulting and Hayley Mills once lived. We skirted to the left of a post and wire fence and then some trees, continuing ahead at a footpath junction to a kissing gate at the crest of the hill.

Through this we turned right on to Ibstone Road, passing the windmill then heading left over a stile by the steep hill sign to follow a wide track downhill between fences in woodland. We left the track at a footpath sign, the footpath initially parallel to the track, which soon veered right and disappeared from our sight. The path descended steeply to emerge in a meadow where we bore half right to merge with a track from the left. Over a stile we continued along the track to reach a lane.

2. We turned right along this narrow country lane, dense hedges alongside, to walk down a beautiful valley, passing Manor Farm, Fingest, with its fine collection of tiled and black-boarded barns and the home of Great Barn Opera. Shortly before the village we passed the iron-railed village pound where stray animals were kept years ago until reclaimed. Past the delightful timber-framed Church Cottage and just before the Old Rectory, which has featured in *Midsomer Murders,* we turned into St Bartholomew's parish churchyard. A much-photographed Norman church in a picturesque valley setting, it is dominated by its great tower with its fourteenth-century saddle-back roof. The nave is narrower and also Norman with a later chancel, the whole rendered outside and in. Well worth the visit in our view.

3. Leaving the church we headed along the diagonal path to the other churchyard kissing gate and turned left to walk past The Chequers Inn, also seen in *Midsomer Murders*, past the barns of Fingest Farm and turned right over a stile beyond to walk alongside a hedge, and then climb towards woods. Over another stile we entered Fingest Wood to follow the clear path through it. Emerging into a meadow we headed half left across it and through a gap beside a field gate, a footpath sign on the post.

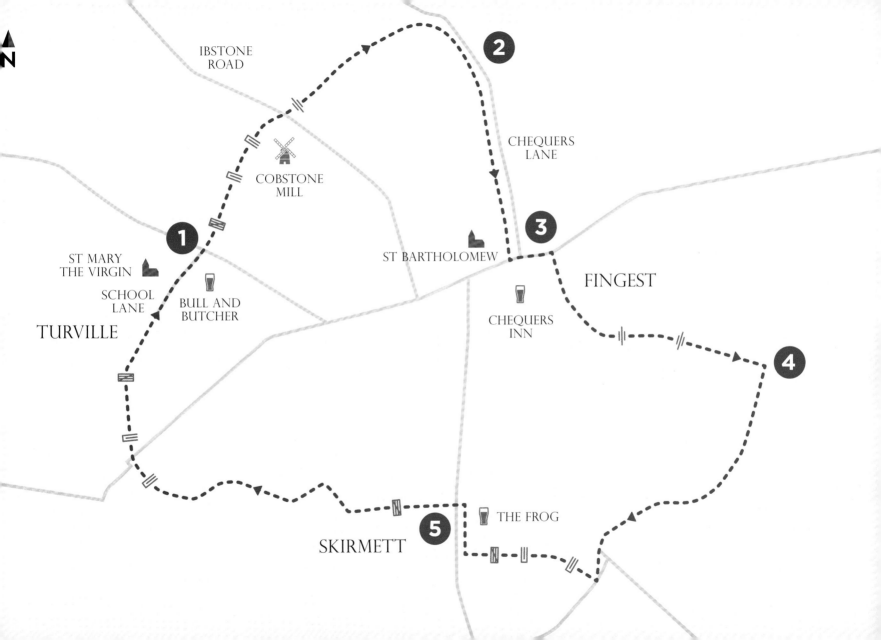

N

IBSTONE ROAD

2

CHEQUERS LANE

COBSTONE MILL

3

ST BARTHOLOMEW

FINGEST

1

ST MARY THE VIRGIN

SCHOOL LANE

BULL AND BUTCHER

CHEQUERS INN

TURVILLE

4

THE FROG

5

SKIRMETT

4. After about 50m we left the track to turn right on to the Chiltern Way, now in Adam's Wood, owned by the Woodland Trust. The path weaves through attractive woodland but we found it easy to follow. Reaching a path junction we headed downhill, a 'CW' sign (Chiltern Way) on a tree to guide us. Emerging from the wood we followed a sunken lane to just before where it met a tarmac lane. Beyond a field gate we went right through a kissing gate and descended a path through a meadow, passed through another kissing gate, and continued ahead across horse gallops, Skirmett village ahead. We headed towards a white bungalow and through a hand gate we passed the village hall to reach Skirmett Road, the village road.

5. For refreshment at The Frog at Skirmett you could go left but we turned right along the road and just past All Saints House we turned left along a metalled track within a lime avenue, crossed the Hamble Brook (it does not always flow) and passed Poynatts Manor on the left. At the end of the fence we passed through a hand gate. The footpath climbs towards woods, a new post and wire fence on our right. Reaching the woods the path bears right along its edge, then at the end bears left within the wood edge up a sunken lane that veers right. The path then weaves within the woods, generally following the contour line.

At a footpath post we bore right to descend on a path to a meadow on the valley floor. We crossed the meadow to a footpath post with more views of Cobstone Mill away to our right. The track passes through a copse with a fenced-off gas installation on our left. Through a hand gate we crossed the lane to a kissing gate to follow the clear path half right across pasture. Reaching the hedge we joined another footpath and bore right along it, passed through a hand gate and descended on a tree-girt path to reach Turville village, noting the 1873 former school seen in a *Midsomer Murders* episode. This is School Lane, which leads back to the village green and the end of a most enjoyable walk sampling the delights of the glorious Hambleden Valley.

Hambleden Brook valley, Turville.

WALK 12 CRICKET AND KITES 5.75 MILES (9.2KM)

Ibstone and Wormsley Park

INTRODUCTION

Starting in the village of Stokenchurch, a much-expanded one in recent years, we pass under the roar of the M40 and are immediately in tranquil countryside, walking on tracks and paths in expansive steep-sided dry valleys and woodland. The fields are mostly arable, swaying with ripened corn when we did the walk. To the west is Wormsley Park with a mix of parkland and fields. It is a delightful walk with a couple of climbs and descents of the chalk ridge upon which straggles the village of Ibstone.

Stokenchurch village grew up on the old Oxford to London coach road, now the A40, and Kings Hotel, formerly the King's Head, was its major inn. The M40 bypassed the village in the 1970s but its motorway junction led to a substantial sprawl of housing estates. Wormsley Park, with its eighteenth-century mansion, is now associated with the Getty family and its cricket ground is a major attraction. The scenery on this walk, though, is quintessentially Chilterns with superb dry valleys and sweeps of beech woods on the slopes.

MIDSOMER COMES TO WORMSLEY

The focus of this walk is Wormsley Park, which can be seen at Point 4 of the route, although there is no public right of way up to the cricket pitch or the house. In winter you might see more with the leaves off the trees. From various points along the valley floor approaching Point 5 and at the junction where the drive bears left, the splendid wide thatched pavilion and the thatched scoreboard hut away to its left come into view. This ground was used for the cricket match in 'Secrets and Spies'. Beyond this, where we turned right on to the path to ascend to the Ibstone ridge once more, is a

Most of the route is dog friendly but in Stokenchurch dogs should be on leads while there are horses in the fields immediately south of the M40.

There are no public toilets so rely on those in the Fleur de Lis in Stokenchurch, provided you buy a drink of course.

Park in the car park in front of the Kings Hotel in Stokenchurch, which has free public parking.

The Fleur de Lis in Stokenchurch, on the route, was welcoming and we had a good lunch and a pint. The Kings Hotel at the very start would be an alternative.

The Kings Hotel has the postcode of HP14 3TA.

Ordnance Survey Explorer Map 171.

pair of cottages, also on the Wormsley Estate, used in 'Talking to the Dead'. Reaching Ibstone, if you continued for half a mile south-east past the cricket ground on the common, you reach Ibstone School, a delightful flint and stone-dressed Victorian school used in 'The Straw Woman' as Midsomer Parva's school. However, this diversion is along a road with no pavement and is not included on this route.

A BIT OF HISTORICAL BACKGROUND

Nowadays Wormsley Park is known for its ownership by the Getty family, its cricket ground, its recently established housing of the renowned Garsington Opera and for Sir Paul's major role in the reintroduction of the red kite into the Chilterns after he bought the estate in 1986.

The estate has a long history though and is recorded as a manor in the thirteenth century. By the sixteenth century it was held by the Scropes, one of whose descendants, Colonel Adam Scrope, signed the death warrant of Charles I and suffered a brutal death (he was hung, drawn and quartered) after the Restoration of Charles II for his pains. In the early eighteenth century the estate passed by marriage to the Fane family, several of whose scions had too keen an interest in horse racing, gambling and fast cars, so the estate had its ups and downs. When Sir Paul Getty bought it the house was virtually derelict and the grounds, park and farms were in a similarly poor state. Now it is all in superb shape, the parkland full of deer and Sir Paul's love of cricket made manifest in the cricket ground where international touring teams and first class counties play. He was introduced to the game, incidentally, by another devotee: Mick Jagger. In the sky above, and all over the Chilterns, one of Sir Paul's most lasting memorials – besides the wall tablet in Lewknor church (Walk 9) – can be seen in the form of the huge numbers of red kites wheeling and mewing above us as we walked Midsomer land. So successful has the project been that these noble birds have been sent all over Britain and their range is now great. It is amazing now to remember that it all started with a mere three chicks, two from Spain and one from Sweden.

THE WALK

1. On another sunny September day with high clouds we started out from the car park in front of the Kings Hotel and headed behind it on to Church Road to visit the surprisingly good parish church of Saints Peter and Paul. I say surprising because the village, apart from its extensive commons, is not particularly prepossessing and surrounded by suburban housing estates. Outside the church is pebble-dashed like any suburban pre-war bungalow, but inside is a complete contrast of whitewashed walls and thirteenth-century arches into the north aisle.

The chancel arch is elaborately enriched with late twelfth-century chevron carvings and in the chancel is a wall memorial to Bartholomew Tipping who died in 1680, now with detail picked out in colour and gold. He founded a free school in the village for a schoolmaster and twelve local boys: no girls, we noted.

Returning to the car park we crossed the A40 at the pedestrian crossing and headed half right towards the Fleur de Lis on the south side of one of the village's many commons. Passing to its left we continued down Coopers Court Road, now briefly within a 1970s housing estate. We crossed Slade Road, now on the Chiltern Way path, and passed through the tunnel under the M40, leaving Stokenchurch behind. Here we took the left fork to a stile. Over this we headed towards the next fork in the farm roads where we bore right to follow the track along the floor of a delightful dry valley, the horse paddocks soon left behind where the track bears left. Here we continued ahead on the footpath, now passing between fields of ripe corn.

Reaching a stile the path entered woodland and curved back and forth along the valley floor amid the beech and pine trees, arrows painted on trees by the admirable Chiltern Society to guide us, although not now following the Chiltern Way itself. We continued past two footpath signs, the first one on the left, the second on the right, but at the third sign we left the valley floor track we had been following to bear right uphill but still in woodland.

2. The track climbed out of the valley, passing under electricity cables. Emerging from the wood we continued ahead and walked alongside a hedge, mostly hazel, before crossing a track and continuing ahead into more woodland, much of it hazel coppice, along a track. Reaching the end of the woods we passed Cholsey Grange, its farm buildings occupied by specialist conservation builders, and passed a field gate to reach the road through Ibstone village. We turned left to pass the cricket pitch carved out of a corner of Ibstone Common and bore right on to Grays Lane passing the somewhat utilitarian cricket pavilion for Ibstone Cricket Club. We passed the nets and children's play area and were now on Ibstone Common proper. The lane bore left but we continued ahead on a metalled track heading for Bellows Cottage. Here we turned right at a footpath sign on to the path along the west edge of the common, butterflies in profusion on the day we walked.

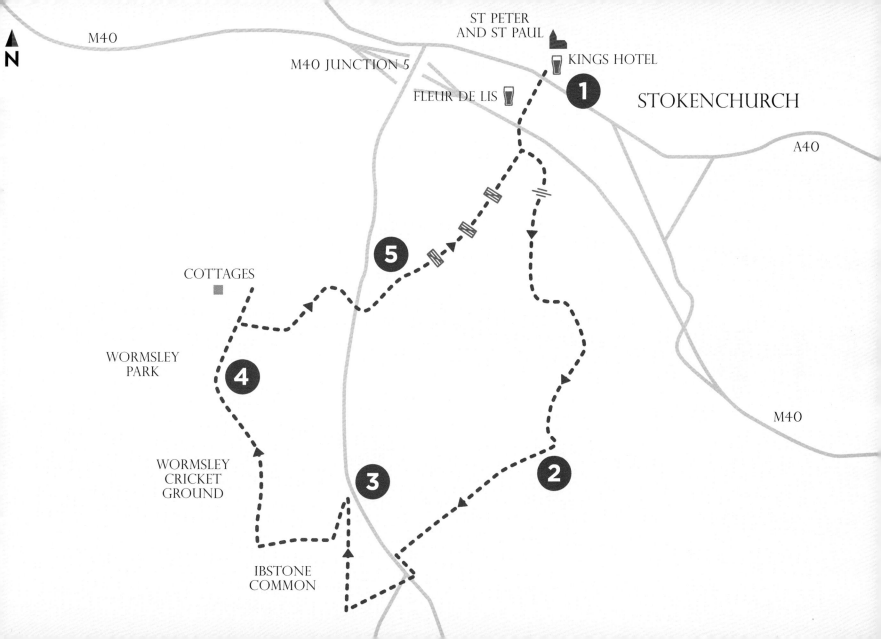

A tree-lined avenue, Wormsley Estate.

3. Reaching a footpath post we bore left, rejoining the Chiltern Way route, and followed the path into the woods and on to the Wormsley Estate. The route is a path worn into a sunken way that descends from the ridge and we continued ahead where the Chiltern Way bore left, painted arrows on the trees making this clear. The path bears right and descends to the valley floor where it joins a grassy track. Away to the left we glimpsed the cricket ground on the last stretch of track before merging with another path.

4. At the junction with a sign reading 'To the Cricket and Opera' the track becomes a surfaced road. The opera is the Garsington Opera, which translated here a couple of years ago to a temporary opera house looking out over Wormsley Park's lake and deer park. It is here that we could most readily view the cricket ground with its thatched pavilion and thatched scoreboard hut, as well as the house up on its hill. The opera house is also to be glimpsed at various points.

We continued along the valley floor road, observing stags with massive antlers within the fenced deer park to our left. Reaching a modern thatched estate cottage colour-washed in yellow ochre at Wellground Farm, we bore right at a footpath sign to climb back on to the wooded ridge. Looking left we could see the black weatherboarding and ornate gable bargeboards of the pair of estate cottages used in 'Talking to the Dead'. At a fork the path bore left to climb steeply and at the crest bore right, becoming a track within a tree belt between fields. Near the road we looked left over a field gate to see the tall landmark of the 1950s Telecom Tower and the thatched lodge cottage at the main entrance to Wormsley Park.

5. At the road we crossed it into woodland and alongside a high fence. At a footpath junction we bore left (there is an arrow on a tree), the fence still alongside for a stretch. We followed the path across a dry valley to a stile. Over this we continued ahead, a cottage to our left, to cross a lane via two hand gates and straight on alongside trees and a hedge. Through another hand gate we continued alongside the hedge, now back on the Chiltern Way, the Telecom Tower away to our left.

Through another hand gate the path descended through a shaw or wood planted on the slope of a dry valley, then climbed alongside a hedge. Reaching an access road to Coopers Court Farm, formerly a dairy farm and a muddy experience to get past, we crossed it. Through a hand gate the path bore half right between post and rail fences to another hand gate. Through this we joined a lane and once again passed beneath the M40 and back to Stokenchurch, lunching well at the Fleur de Lis.

Footpath and farmland, Stokenchurch.

Sunday limited-overs cricket at one of the most beautiful cricket grounds in the country.

A pair of cottages on the Wormsley Estate used in 'Talking to the Dead'.

BOTTLE KILNS, BRICKS AND BOND 4.25 MILES (6.8KM)

Nettlebed

INTRODUCTION

This is a most enjoyable and scenic walk and mostly on field and woodland paths and tracks, apart from quiet lanes around Crocker End and, obviously, the High Street in Nettlebed itself. The only livestock on the route when we walked it were a couple of ponies in a paddock west of Highmoor, apart from dogs being walked and glimpses of deer in the woods.

The route combines delightful beech woods and coppices with field paths, while the deep dry valley on the western part of the route provides fine open scenery as well.

MIDSOMER COMES TO NETTLEBED AND CROCKER END

Nettlebed and Crocker End, its eastern hamlet, featured in several episodes. Crocker End has a village green and, like The Lee, is a popular type of location for *Midsomer Murders*, evoking village life. It became Midsomer Mallow in 'Judgement Day' and Midsomer Parva in 'Shot at Dawn' and was also used in 'Maid in Splendour'.

Nettlebed itself featured in other episodes with the interior shots for 'Dance with the Dead' using the village hall, a fine 1912 Arts and Crafts building erected as a working men's club. The exterior also featured in 'The Magician's Nephew', as did views in the High Street. The interior of The White Hart was used as the Maid in Splendour pub for that episode and the village itself appeared in 'Death and Dust', in which a furniture and antique shop became a home furnishings store.

Joyce Grove, the Sue Ryder home in large grounds south of the village, became Bledlow Manor in 'Blood Wedding', a slightly odd name as the real Bledlow Manor is the name of Lord Carrington's house in Bledlow (Walk 6).

 Much of the route is dog friendly but in Nettlebed dogs should be on leads.

 No public toilets so rely on those in the pub and the cafe in Nettlebed.

 Park on the roads near the kiln and near the bus stop just east of the village centre.

 The White Hart was used in a *Midsomer Murders* episode and is excellent but there is also The Field Cafe and delicatessen at the Nettlebed Village Shop, in the flint-built Victorian former school building.

 Park near the old kiln (the postcode for The Old Kiln is RG9 5BA).

 Ordnance Survey Explorer 171.

A BIT OF HISTORICAL BACKGROUND

At the centre of Nettlebed is a curious tall brick structure but the cul de sac named The Old Kiln rather gives the game away. This is the last surviving 'bottle kiln' from a local industry that grew up in the Middle Ages. Nettlebed was a significant centre for brick and tile making and an early one at that, supplying

Mist and the morning sun.

thousands of bricks for Wallingford Castle in 1365 (Walk 19) and for Abingdon Abbey and Stonor Park in the fifteenth century (Walk 10). Kilns also existed in Crocker Green and Soundess, north-east of Crocker Green. The industry grew mightily and there was even a tramway from Windmill Hill to carry brick clay to the kilns in the village. Competition with cheap bricks from Staffordshire and elsewhere led to rapid decline by 1900 and the last firings were in 1938. So as you walk remember that this was an industrial area; perhaps that is why it had a working men's club in the High Street (now the village hall).

THE WALK

1. On a crisp and sunny December day we set out from near the Bottle Kiln, having looked at the pudding stones on the verge near the bus shelter. We had encountered these conglomerates (whose origins date back to the great ice ages) on an earlier walk, in Princes Risborough (Walk 7). We headed east along the lane towards the Chapel Lane sign. Here we continued ahead, not turning left into Chapel Lane, then passing Mulberry House. Now within the wooded common we continued ahead at a road junction and shortly bore right, signed Crocker End. After a few yards we bore right on to a footpath along the south side of the grassy common or village green at Crocker End.

2. This common was seen in two episodes, renamed Midsomer Mallow in 'Judgement Day' and Midsomer Parva in 'Shot at Dawn'. The path reached a lane where we bore right with No. 23, a timber-framed cottage, on our left and an old granary on stone and brick 'staddles' to our right, these being intended to prevent rats climbing into the granary to raid its grain bins. At Old Tiles we bore right to descend on a lane that curved between pastures and then climbed out of the valley. At the curiously named 'Catslip' hamlet we continue ahead into the trees of the common, the lane reaching the busy A4130 to Henley.

3. Across the road we followed the path ahead through the mainly beech trees of the wooded Lower Common, the ground still golden russet with autumn's fallen leaves. Painted arrows on trees marked our route and we noted a woodland boundary bank on our left at some points. The path bore right at an arrow,

Clockwise from top left: Walking through Nettlebed Woods; a plaque in Nettlebed acknowledging the Fleming family's commitment to the village, though no mention of Ian Fleming, the creator of James Bond; the interior of The White Hart in Nettlebed was used as the Maid in Splendour after its modernisation; Nettlebed's last kiln; a moss-covered stump in Nettlebed Woods.

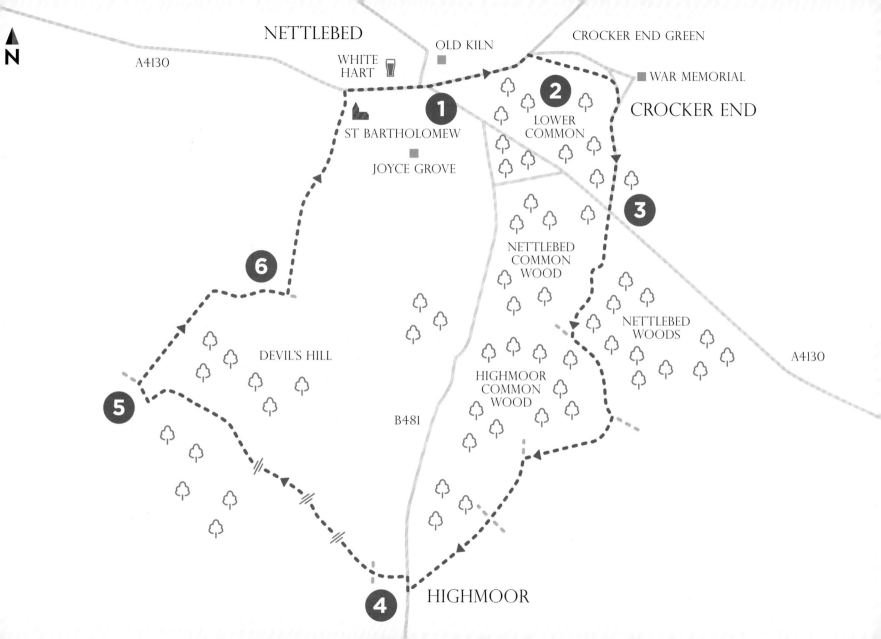

and then left to descend to the valley floor. Here we bore left along a track, marked as a 'Restricted Byway'. It opened up to the left with a field and, at a path junction, we bore right up a track, now with a field on our right and a more open wooded glade to our left. We climbed out of the valley and at a fork bore right. Now with pasture fields beyond the hedges, we passed a Neo-Georgian house, Merrimoles, and bore left at a footpath post on to a track. It joined a tarmac lane amid the beeches and oaks of Highmoor Common, the low winter sun casting long tree shadows around us. At a cross paths we continued ahead and passed a neat, late seventeenth-century timber-framed cottage, Tudor Cottage, with painted brick infill, its name a little hopeful in dating terms.

4. Reaching the road, the B481, we turned right, then left at a footpath sign which goes past to the right of Green Man and Appletree cottages before bearing half right into woodland. At another footpath post we bore right, crossed an access drive and just before The Cottage turned right, signed 'Heath Walks'. This is a courtesy path that avoids going straight through the garden and courtyard of The Cottage, which is actually the public footpath route but must be quite trying in summer.

This alternative route weaves through a young copse with a holly and other evergreen understorey to reach a stile. Over this we continued ahead alongside the hedge in a pony paddock to another stile. Beyond this the permissive path rejoins the statutory footpath and we continued within a beech wood where we watched a herd of deer leaping through the trees. The path goes down to a stile and over this we descended in pasture to the valley floor. Another stile took us into the edge of a wood, Nott Wood, and the path bore right along the valley floor, fir trees amid the hazel coppices. These gave way to beech trees, the route marked by white arrows on some trees to guide us as the path bore left to climb out of the valley, then wound along the more level crest. We continued curving left where paths merged at a footpath post to reach the woodland edge.

5. At the wood margin we turned right on to a bridleway and, approaching Howberrywood, bore right on to a tarmac track that continued alongside the wood that clothes the splendidly named Devil's Hill. Soon the track descended into the dry valley where we followed the road as it curves round and then went right on to a bridleway, close to a farm access road in the edge of the woods, in fact a sunken way.

6. At the top of the slope we turned left back on to the lane and followed it northwards over the crest with a hedge on our right. Nearing the outskirts of Nettlebed we walked along the path behind the churchyard wall to reach the main road, the A4130, where we turned right to walk through the village. The church is a disappointing one with only the base of the medieval tower surviving a somewhat uninspiring Victorian rebuild. However, the High Street has some fine Georgian buildings, several of them former coaching inns, and we were also back in *Midsomer Murders* country with the Nettlebed Village Club and The White Hart having had both their interiors used in episodes. We saw this as a good enough reason to have a sandwich and a drink in The White Hart before the end of the walk. Opposite the kiln are the gates to Joyce Grove, a substantial Jacobean-style brick and stone mansion of 1908 and now a Sue Ryder home that became 'Bledlow Manor' in 'Blood Wedding'.

'Dance with the Dead' used the village hall, a fine 1912 Arts and Crafts building erected as a working men's club.

POOHSTICKS, CLUMPS AND AN ABBEY

WALK 14 THE RED LION CONSUMES THE GOOSE 6.5 MILES (10.4KM)

Britwell Salome

INTRODUCTION

This walk is the second longest in the book, being 6.5 miles, but takes in some superb Chiltern scenery with deep-cut dry valleys, wooded hills and sheep-cropped hill pasture. It starts from the village of Britwell Salome, not to be confused with Brightwell Baldwin on Walk 18 or with Berrick Salome not far away. En route are two good village churches: Swyncombe's is particularly picturesquely situated, high in the Chilterns with sheep-cropped pastures beyond the churchyard. The route is almost entirely on footpaths and tracks with roads only in Britwell Salome. The only livestock on the route when we walked it were sheep in the fields east of Swyncombe, seen from within the churchyard.

The route combines large downland fields of arable, wooded valleys and coombes with a small village and an upland parish with only a couple of houses near the remote church.

MIDSOMER COMES TO BRITWELL SALOME

The village has been used for one grand location and one farmhouse-type location. Britwell House, a rather grand early eighteenth-century red-brick mansion to the south-west of the village is seen from the track to its south-east and was used in two episodes. In 'Birds of Prey' it was used as the Edmontons house and in 'Death in Chorus' it became the Armitages house.

Just before the end of the walk we passed Bartlett's, an early eighteenth-century farmhouse, which became Naomi Sinclair's home also in 'Birds of Prey'.

Almost all of the route is dog friendly apart from in Britwell Salome itself where dogs should be on leads.

No public toilets so rely on those in the Red Lion.

Park in Turner's Green at the west end of Britwell Salome, perhaps near the Red Lion pub, though space is limited (or ask permission to use the pub car park).

The Red Lion pub in Britwell Salome does very good food but is closed Mondays. For a few years it was called The Goose.

The postcode for the Red Lion is OX49 5LG.

Ordnance Survey Explorer 171.

A BIT OF HISTORICAL BACKGROUND

The rather romantic name of Britwell Salome has its suffix shared with nearby Berrick Salome and probably comes from the surname of the family who held both manors in the Middle Ages, the De Sulhams. Disappointingly it does not relate to the daughter of King Herod who danced for him and as a reward was given the head of John the Baptist.

The great house is, of course, Britwell House south-west of the village, set in extensive grounds and featured in two *Midsomer Murders* episodes. The Roman Catholic Simeons had acquired the manor in 1600, John Simeon marrying into the prominent local Catholic Stonor family of Stonor Park. Britwell House was built in the 1720s (there are rainwater heads dated '1728') for the baronet, Sir Edward Simeon, who had a second major building surge in the years before his death in 1768 when he added a sumptuously furnished oval chapel. He was a bachelor and amateur architect: indeed he designed the chapel himself and the column of 1764 as a memorial to his parents. You can see the tall column topped by an urn in the views on the walk. It seems likely, though, that the house was designed by William Townsend, a busy Oxford architect. Its brick facade with stone dressings and a central pediment is beautifully proportioned and, like so many houses of this period, much plainer outside than in.

Swyncombe farmland.

THE WALK

1. We set off on a crisp and sunny day in early January, the low sun giving a rich intensity to the landscape and the colour of trees and buildings.

Walking past the Red Lion, an eighteenth-century building, and beyond Red Lion Farm, we crossed the road and passed through a hand gate to enter a track that runs parallel to the road. After a kissing gate we continued ahead across a cattle grid and bore left to pass a grain store on our right. We descended to a field gate, and through this kept alongside a fence to the next field gate. We turned left along a lane, a tree-girt pond on our right, continuing along this lane past Lower Farm and its roadside farm buildings, a pyramid-roofed granary at the end. Ahead is the church with its bellcote on the west gable and beyond to its right the early Georgian former rectory: a delightful view.

2. The Victorian architect, Charles Buckeridge, rebuilt the church of St Nicholas in the 1860s. He did reuse a Norman nave doorway, but for some reason relocated it to the chancel, and also reused the chancel arch. The plain cup-shaped thirteenth-

View across the Thames Valley to Wittenham Clumps and Didcot Power Station.

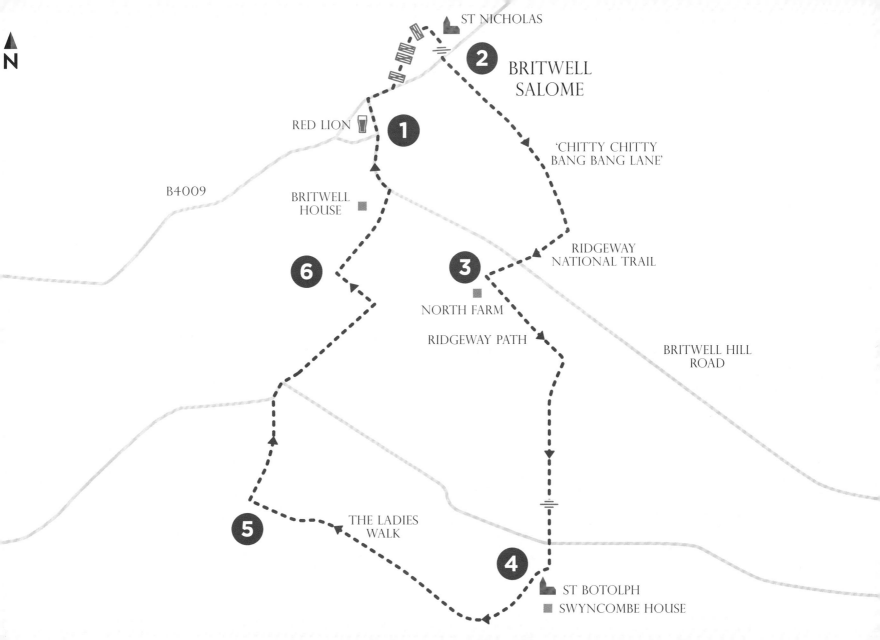

N

ST NICHOLAS

2

BRITWELL
SALOME

RED LION

1

'CHITTY CHITTY
BANG BANG LANE'

B4009

BRITWELL
HOUSE

6

RIDGEWAY
NATIONAL TRAIL

3

NORTH FARM

RIDGEWAY PATH

BRITWELL HILL
ROAD

5

THE LADIES
WALK

4

ST BOTOLPH

SWYNCOMBE HOUSE

century font and its seventeenth-century wooden cover survived also and some earlier wall memorials. Above the chancel arch a stone plaque records the rebuilding for the then rector, J. T. Johnson, but only owns up to rebuilding the chancel.

The Old Rectory is partly seventeenth century but was remodelled twice, firstly for James Stopes in about 1670 and then for his son, also named James, in the early eighteenth century. These rectors were members of a dynasty of clergymen who held the living from the seventeenth to the late eighteenth century and rebuilt the rectory in a style fitting for a landowning gentleman clergyman.

From the churchyard gate we crossed to a hand gate, then continued ahead alongside a fence, a castellated gate lodge away to our right. Over a stile we turned right to briefly follow the main road before bearing left at Cooper's Farm on to a lane. This bridleway – nicknamed 'Chitty Chitty Bang Bang Lane' because it was used in that film – climbs towards the Chiltern escarpment and meets the Ridgeway National Trail, here following the Icknield Way. We turned right to follow the Ridgeway from where we could see Britwell House and its monumental column away to the west.

Britwell House – in 'Birds of Prey' it was used as the Edmontons house and in 'Death in Chorus' it became the Armitages house.

Beautiful red kites.

3. At North Farm we bore left, still on the Ridgeway, skirting to the left of farm buildings. The path then climbs steeply up the Chiltern escarpment and up through woodland before descending to cross a dry valley. We passed through a kissing gate to cross a road and continued ahead along a lane, signposted 'St Botolphs, Swyncombe'. The lane descends and where it bears right we went left through a kissing gate to visit Swyncombe church, enjoying the pastoral landscape beyond the churchyard.

4. The church is a picturesque Norman one, typical of the hamlets of the Chilterns: small, intimate and isolated. Built in flint with sparing use of stone for window frames and doors, it has a nave and apsidal chancel (that is semi-circular in plan). Apart from window alterations nothing much changed here until careful restorations took place in the nineteenth century and in 1914 a late medieval-style timber chancel screen was added designed by Walter Topper. But it is the setting that is so wonderful and evocative. It was held by the great Norman abbey of Bec-Hellouin until 1404 and must have been built while the monks owned the manor and the parish church.

It obviously served as, in effect, the lord of the manor's chapel as much as a parish church. Swyncombe House, the manor house, was near the church but only its early nineteenth-century stable block survives. The current house dates only from the 1980s, having replaced one built in the 1840s in a Jacobean style. This in turn replaced the sixteenth-century house that had superseded the medieval one but sadly that rebuild burned down in 1814.

Back through the kissing gate we continued along the Ridgeway National Trail alongside a close-boarded fence, then ahead along the valley floor. Where the Ridgeway National Trail goes left we continued along the valley track. At a 'Private' sign we bore left on to a path through a copse, then alongside a hedge through open country on what is marked on the OS map as 'Ladies Walk'. We continued alongside the hedge where it bore left towards and through a tree belt, soon passing the gates to Ewelme Down House to join its drive. We followed this to a footpath crossroads.

5. Here we bore right on to a bridleway track, a hedge on our left. The path bore left, a hedge now on our right as far as a road. Here we turned right along it and then, where the road bore right, we continued ahead on a track, a beech wood on our right, the track following the parish boundary. Beyond the end of the woods we turned left along a track, Britwell House ahead, and continued gently downhill to a T-junction of tracks.

6. Here we turned right along the track, now with views of Britwell House on our left, many kites wheeling away above us and the arable field to our right. Reaching a lane we turned left to follow it back into Britwell Salome village, Bartlett's (Naomi Sinclair's house) the second house of the village on the corner of a lane that contains most of the village's older houses. Just before reaching the Red Lion we passed a 'tin tabernacle'-style village hall in green-painted corrugated iron, a gift from the Misses Smith of Britwell House, given in the early 1900s. These 'tin tabernacles' with vaguely Gothic detail turn up all over the place and in the former British Empire where they were exported as 'flat packs' in ship's holds.

WALK 15 ONE EYE AND HALF A MOON 3.75 MILES (6KM)

Cuxham and Brightwell Baldwin

INTRODUCTION

This walk has in its modest length two fine villages, the parkland of a country house and a watermill mentioned in the Domesday Book. It is mostly on field paths and tracks, apart from the village streets and a stretch of road at the north end of the route. The only livestock on the route when we walked it were cattle and calves in one of Manor Farm's fields, secure behind a stone field wall.

 Much of the route is dog friendly but in the villages and on the road around Cutt Mill dogs should be on leads.

 No public toilets so rely on those in the pubs.

 Park in Cuxham on the short lane to the parish church and Manor Farm or in the village, although space is limited.

 There is a choice of two outstanding pubs, the quality of whose cuisine is known far and wide, so you are spoilt for choice: the Lord Nelson in Brightwell Baldwin and the Half Moon in Cuxham.

 The postcode for Marlbrook Cottage at the church lane/main street junction is OX49 5NH.

 Ordnance Survey Explorer 171.

The route combines sweeping and expansive open country and villages with a rich history and of considerable attractiveness. For us the parkland to Brightwell Park was the most impressive landscape.

MIDSOMER COMES TO BRIGHTWELL BALDWIN

Although the walk starts in Cuxham, *Midsomer Murders* appears not to have visited this very attractive village with its well-known Half Moon pub and the stream, the Marl Brook, running alongside its main street. Instead Brightwell Baldwin featured in several episodes and the parish church of St Bartholomew was used for two funerals, one in 'Destroying Angel', the other in 'A Talent for Life'. The Lord Nelson opposite the church is, of course, seen in these funerals episodes, a pub renowned for its superb food and brought back from the dead in a reverse *Midsomer* way in 1971 when it reopened after having been closed for sixty-five years, apparently initially because of estate workers' overindulgence. A further episode featured Brightwell Baldwin when the cameras followed a woman cycling through the village in 'Judgement Day'. Brightwell Baldwin Cottage, the one with a disconcerting dummy of a yokel in its porch, featured in 'The Glitch' as Melanie and Tom Jeffers' house.

A BIT OF HISTORICAL BACKGROUND

Cuxham was and still is largely owned by Merton College, Oxford, as were many manors in a wide swathe of country around Oxford. Its church was largely rebuilt in the late seventeenth century, although its tower west door has a reused Norman doorway with intricate foliage capitals and graffiti with dates scratched on the doorjambs in the 1790s. The old rectory is a grander building, rebuilt in 1823 by the new rector to suit his social status as a gentleman. The village stream, the Marl Brook, adds to its picturesqueness, particularly in March when its banks are glorious with daffodils.

Brightwell Baldwin has a superb church, which sits on the south side of the great park to Brightwell Park, also known as Brightwell House. Probably emparked out of the village fields in the late thirteenth century, the park grew over the years and reached its present extent after 1802, possibly landscaped by the great garden designer Humphrey Repton. The park is divided in two by a long, sinuous lake with the mansion site in the western half, along with a seventeenth-century dovecote for the lord of the manor's table, a survivor of the earlier manor buildings. The old house was somewhere near the present one but in 1788 it was destroyed by fire and a new house and stable block were built soon after for William Lowndes Stone. You will look in vain for a mansion, though, as only the shell of the ground-floor walls survive adjacent to the stable blocks, long converted to dwellings. The fine Georgian mansion became dilapidated and was largely pulled down in 1947.

THE WALK

1. Again we were lucky with the weather, setting off in cold March sunshine with rain due by mid-morning. From beside the church we headed south and away from the village, past the farm buildings of Manor Farm, the house an Edwardian rebuild after a fire destroyed the old farmhouse. At the end of the pasture field on our right we left the track and bore right on to a footpath alongside a fence and hedge with good views across Cuxham and a string of medieval fishponds west of Manor Farm. The old rectory was covered in scaffolding but is a substantial building dating from 1823 when the new vicar, Francis Rowden the younger, became rector and rebuilt it more in keeping with his status as a gentleman rector.

We followed this grassy path beside a long arable field and at the end turned right on to a bridle path, in fact Turner's Lane, the old route between Brightwell Baldwin and Britwell Salome. We followed this as it descended between tree belts to a road.

Marl Brook and the village of Cuxham.

An avenue of cedars in Brightwell Park.

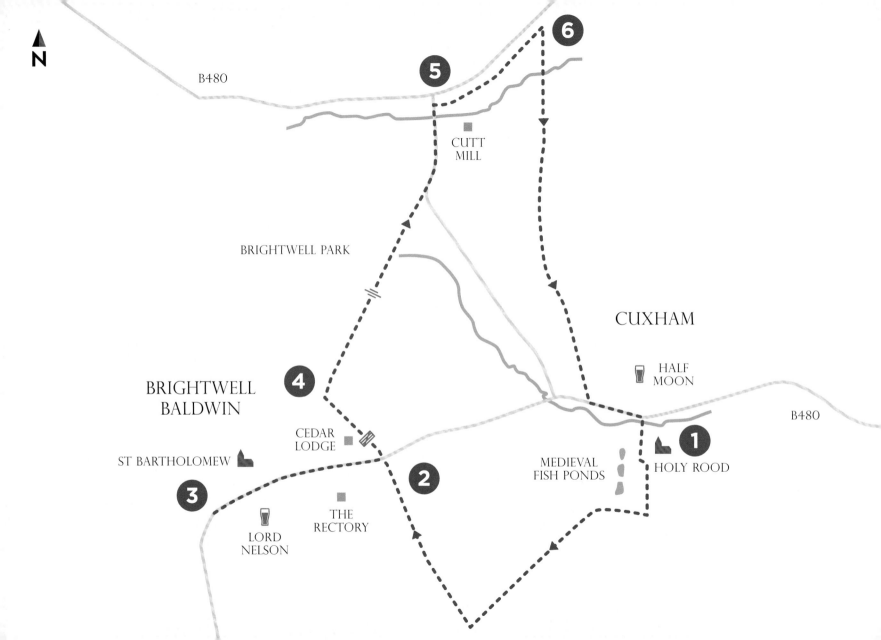

N

B480

⑤

⑥

CUTT
MILL

BRIGHTWELL PARK

CUXHAM

HALF
MOON

BRIGHTWELL
BALDWIN

④

B480

CEDAR
LODGE

ST BARTHOLOMEW

②

①

MEDIEVAL
FISH PONDS

HOLY ROOD

③

THE
RECTORY

LORD
NELSON

2. At the road we bore left into Brightwell Baldwin, passing on the left the Old Rectory, a stuccoed house of the 1790s with an in and out carriageway and a rather sophisticated facade, the ground-floor sashes and entrance set within semi-circular arches. Past this we looked right to the cress-filled lake of Brightwell Park winding towards a parkland bridge built across the lake soon after 1802. The parkland is a pretty impressive example of an early nineteenth-century country house's picturesque landscape. We continued through the village with its stone and brick dressed cottages and farmhouses, one, Brightwell Baldwin Cottage, with a dummy dressed as a yokel staring blankly out from within its modern glazed porch.

3. Opposite the church is the Lord Nelson pub with elaborate, foliage-carved windows and door frame, which must presumably owe something to its original role as the inn serving the big house where eighteenth and nineteenth-century

visitors could be put up. The church opposite, its churchyard set higher than the street, is usually open during the day and is a most rewarding one for 'church crawlers' quite apart from its role in *Midsomer Murders* episodes. Besides some outstanding funerary monuments in the north-east chapel, there is a good collection of fourteenth and fifteenth-century stained glass in many of the windows, as well as a pretty 1843 barrel organ designed to look like a chamber organ, and a Jacobean pulpit. To the north of the churchyard we saw the remains of Brightwell Park mansion next to the surviving stable block, now houses.

From the church we retraced our steps through the village back to the bridleway at Point 2 where we bore left. However, there is a permissive path by Cedar Lodge, the east lodge to Brightwell Park, named for obvious reasons when you look into the park beyond. We went through a hand gate to follow the path, which heads diagonally down an avenue of vast cedar trees, the Cedar Avenue,

A patriotic pub notice, the Lord Nelson.

Brightwell country lane in which the cameras followed a woman cycling through the village in 'Judgement Day'.

A disconcerting dummy of a yokel in a porch featured in 'The Glitch' as Melanie and Tom Jeffers' house.

planted soon after 1802. On our right the parkland is corrugated by medieval ridge and furrow so this area was incorporated in the park, having previously been the village's open fields. Possibly they were 'enclosed' in 1802 when an Enclosure Act was passed or perhaps this area had already been taken out of the villagers' common fields by earlier 'emparking' as the park has a long history.

The Lord Nelson.

4. The permissive path passed by a signpost with a direction arrow painted on it to a path junction where we turned right to head for another similar post, fine views of the mansion to our left and of the seventeenth-century stone dovecote further north, both beyond the long, landscaped lake. We continued on this bearing towards a copse and crossed a stile to rejoin the path that runs northwards outside the park. Passing through the copse the path becomes a pretty green lane and merges with the road to Cuxham. Here we bore left along the road and at the bend we turned right at Cuttmill Cottages on to a more minor road signed 'Stoke Talmage and Tetsworth'.

5. Past a copse we saw the painted weatherboarding of Cutt Mill and its timber and brick outbuildings, one of three mills in Cuxham noted in the Domesday Book, although one had gone by the thirteenth century. The other mill was in the village but, being owned by Wallingford Priory, Merton College (who owned most of Cuxham) developed Cutt Mill to avoid paying milling fees to the priory. The current buildings, though, are eighteenth and nineteenth century and it ceased milling in the 1890s. Beyond the mill the wide and overgrown streambed is the remains of the mill's header pond where water was dammed to give a good 'head' of water to drive the water wheel.

6. At a footpath sign we turned right, through the hedge, and crossed new pasture to a footbridge across the stream, continuing half right across further new pasture. At a tree-girt spring-fed pond set in a deep hollow and full of watercress, we bore left alongside a hedged post and wire fence, the rain now having started.

We passed an eighteenth-century timber-framed cottage then reached Cuxham village where, across the Marl Brook stream with its weeping willow and daffodils blooming, we turned left to walk along the main street, the stream soon on our right protected by its white-painted railings. College Farm, a white-painted house on the right, refers, of course, to Merton College which owned the manor and the village for centuries.

We continued past the turning to the church to have lunch in The Half Moon before ending the walk, the pub's unusual name probably a reference to the crest of the seventeenth-century Gregory family who were tenants of the manor farm in the seventeenth century.

POOHSTICKS, CLUMPS AND AN ABBEY 4.5 MILES (7.2KM)

Dorchester and Little Wittenham

INTRODUCTION

This walk is packed with history in its 4.5 miles: an Iron Age town and an Iron Age hill fort, a Roman town, a cathedral founded in Anglo-Saxon times and the seat of a vast bishopric that stretched from the Thames to the River Humber, not to mention the medieval (and later) architecture than fills the town. From the flat country bounded by the rivers Thame and Thames, the route crosses into what used to be Berkshire to climb 230ft (70m) to the tops of two hills, one topped by the ramparts and ditches of a powerful Iron Age hill fort. Little Wittenham

Cattle grazing on the Thames Path National Trail.

 The route is dog friendly apart from in Dorchester or if sheep are grazing the Clumps.

 Public toilets are adjacent to the car park in Bridge End.

 Park in the public car park at Bridge End, near the bridge over the River Thame.

 Where else but The George Hotel, which features in several *Midsomer Murders* episodes and does good food and bar snacks?

 The postcode for houses adjacent to the Bridge End car park is OX10 7JR.

 Ordnance Survey Explorer 170.

church, nestled below the Clumps, contains some fine monuments. The route outside Dorchester itself is almost entirely on field paths and tracks. Sheep were grazing the fields on the Wittenham Clumps when we walked the route.

The route combines flat river-valley fields and meadows together with downland and woodland on two steep chalk hills that can be seen for miles around.

93

MIDSOMER COMES TO DORCHESTER

Midsomer Murders visited Dorchester on Thames quite frequently and The George Hotel, a fine coaching inn of about 1500, featured as the Maid in Splendour in the episode of that name and as The Feathers Hotel in 'The House in the Woods'. The Fleur de Lys became The Devington Arms in 'Master Class' and the cottage next door, The Pigeons, became the Butterball Tea Rooms in 'Small Mercies' while The White Hart Hotel was used in the same episode. Several other houses and cottages featured in various episodes, including 'Things That Go Bump in the Night' and 'Dance with the Dead' while the abbey and its museum have featured several times, including in 'Master Class' and 'The Night of the Stag'.

A BIT OF HISTORICAL BACKGROUND

The old walled Roman town at Dorchester was presumably still recognisable when King Cynegils of Wessex gave it to St Birinus after his baptism here in AD 634. Birinus, a missionary sent to the heathen Saxons by Pope Honorius I, became

The Thames Path National Trail.

The River Thame meets the Isis, the River Thames in Oxfordshire, and they flow as one towards London.

bishop of a vast diocese covering most of southern England. This was a short-lived phase as the cathedral was moved to Winchester in the late seventh century. Dorchester rose again in the late ninth century when it became the seat of a bishopric serving most of the kingdom of Mercia. Nothing of the Anglo-Saxon bishops' churches survives from before the seat of the bishopric was moved by William the Conqueror north from the banks of the Thames to Lincoln in 1072.

After seventy years in limbo the abbey was re-founded by Alexander, Bishop of Lincoln, in 1140. Presumably the new abbey used the Anglo-Saxon church until it was rebuilt in the late twelfth century. The new abbey church was relatively plain and had no aisles but later the chancel was rebuilt and enlarged in a more sumptuous style and a south aisle added to the nave, which is wider than the nave itself. The most remarkable feature though is the Tree of Jesse window with the tracery treated like the branches of the tree and the descendants of Jesse in stained glass dated from about 1310 'standing' on the branches. Outside, the only remaining abbey building, the Guest House, now houses the museum.

THE WALK

1. From the car park in Bridge End we walked to the abbey church and then continued along the High Street, passing the George Hotel on the left with The White Hart Hotel opposite.

2. We left the High Street, turning left down Malthouse Lane before turning right alongside a charming terrace of thatched cottages, their render mostly white-painted but with one standing out in pink. At the end of the path we turned left along a lane, passing Orchard Cottage, No. 26. At the allotments we bore right at the footpath sign to 'Day's Lock' and followed the footpath between arable fields, the Wittenham Clumps ahead and Didcot Power Station in the distance.

3. We reached the massive ramparts and ditches that formed the north boundary of the Iron Age oppidum or 'town', now known as Dyke Hills, with rivers forming the other three boundaries, and bore right parallel to them. We continued ahead

Day's Lock on the River Thames.

across a track and shortly the path took us left through the ramparts. Now we were in the area of the 'town' and continued to a hand gate. Through this we headed towards the footbridge over the Thames, Day's Lock to our right.

Through a hand gate we crossed the pretty river bridge, passed a former Thames Conservancy lock-keeper's cottage, dated 1924, then another two bridges to walk into Little Wittenham and visit its church.

4. Little Wittenham used to be called 'Abbot's Wittenham' as it was owned by Abingdon Abbey and St Michael's church was then known as St Faith's. The chief glory of the interior (it is usually open to visitors) is the Dunch monuments of about 1612 in the tower. There are two alabaster effigies, Sir William awkwardly raised on his elbow and his wife on a lower 'shelf', flanked by obelisks and with their children carved in relief below. An oddly cramped location now but they were originally in a family chapel off the chancel, demolished years ago. There are good memorial brasses also, one to a Tudor William Dunch and his wife, and a rather good canopied tomb in the chancel to Geoffrey Kidwelly who died in 1483.

The tranquillity of the churchyard, however, was rudely interrupted by helicopters flying noisily from nearby RAF Benson. Crossing the lane we went through a hand gate, past an Earth Trust totem pole and headed towards the Wittenham Clumps. Through another hand gate we climbed steeply to a viewpoint marker where we went left alongside the wooded hilltop, the path curving alongside it. Then we bore left across the neck of the ridge, to a hand gate to enter Castle Hill. We took the right fork and climbed steps on to the open grassland of the summit, a copse and a seat on our right.

This hill is surrounded by Iron Age ramparts and ditches but there seems little excavated evidence of large-scale settlement so it might have been a camp for emergencies, gatherings, burials or storage (there were evidently many grain storage pits and burials found). A smaller and earlier Bronze Age enclosure pre-dated the Iron Age one.

At the east end of the central copse is a bronze plaque and a decayed remnant of a beech tree upon which a poem was carved in 1844–45 by one Joseph Tubb of Warborough Green, a maltster who had wished to become a wood carver. Sadly the tree is decidedly fallen, dead and rotting away; we could still make out some of the lettering, but it won't be around for long.

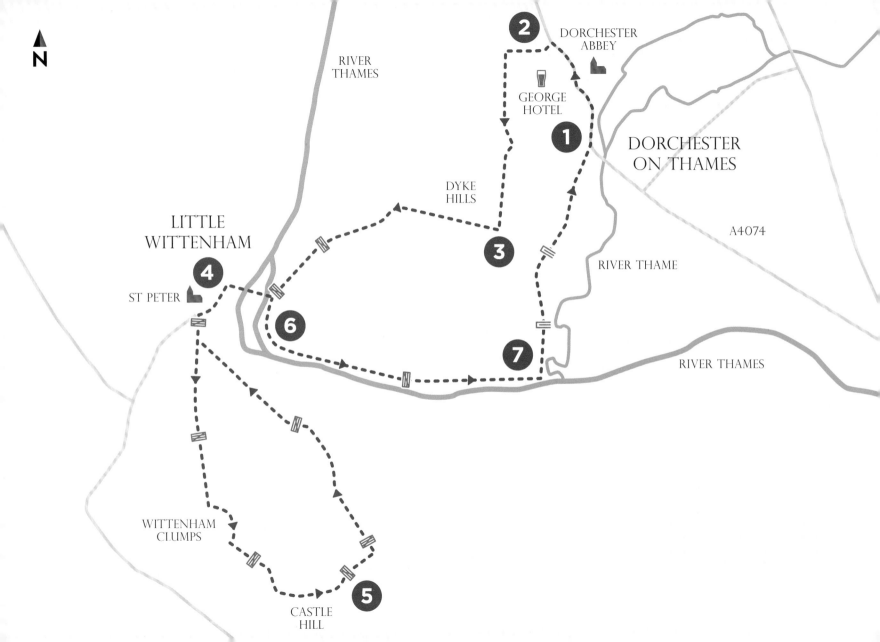

N

DORCHESTER
ON THAMES

A4074

RIVER
THAMES

DORCHESTER
ABBEY

GEORGE
HOTEL

DYKE
HILLS

RIVER THAME

RIVER THAMES

LITTLE
WITTENHAM

ST PETER

WITTENHAM
CLUMPS

CASTLE
HILL

The interior of the George in Dorchester was used as the Maid in Splendour before its modernisation.

5. Having enjoyed the views on this cloudy but clear October day, we descended in the direction of Dorchester and re-crossed the ramparts to a hand gate. Through this the path bears left, then descended the hill alongside woodland on our left, an arable field to our right. About halfway down we went left through a hand gate to follow the path ahead through the woods. We merged with a path from the left and climbed out of a valley but before reaching the crest we bore right on the path that continued through the woods. At a path junction we bore left and through a hand gate left the woods behind. We headed half left across a field to return to Little Wittenham and re-crossed the River Thames.

6. Little Wittenham Bridge's claim to fame is its use in the annual World Poohsticks Championships, which were started here (not the real bridge in A.A. Milne's Sussex) in 1984 by the then lock-keeper, Lynn David. Over the bridge we went sharp left to the riverbank and then left again to pass beneath the bridge and through a hand gate. We were now following the Thames Path National Trail along the riverbank, passing through a further hand gate.

7. Before reaching another hand gate and a bridge we bore left. This is the confluence of the River Thame, a river we see on several of these walk routes, with the Thames. We headed north following the path that runs briefly parallel to the Thame before it meanders away to our right. Through a kissing gate we passed the somewhat more eroded east end of Dyke Hills ramparts, and an old Second World War pillbox. Was this an attempt to defend Dorchester from German invasion, reviving the defensive role of the Dyke Hills, we wondered?

Through a kissing gate we left the pastoral riverbank environs and walked alongside a hedge, the muddy path running parallel to a large arable field. We continued ahead towards a thatched cottage, passing to its right and returning to Dorchester on a metalled lane. At the end of the lane we bore right, then left to pass St Birinus' Roman Catholic church, built in 1849 and dedicated to the first Anglo-Saxon missionary to these parts. We had now reached the car park at the end of the walk but we retraced our steps for a well-deserved bar snack in The George Hotel.

Dorchester cottages, popular in Midsomer Murders, *including 'Things That Go Bump in the Night' and 'Dance with the Dead'.*

Days Lock on the River Thames.

WALK 17 A CHAUCER IN THE CHILTERNS 4.5 MILES (7.2KM)

Ewelme

INTRODUCTION

This walk very much focuses on the delightful village of Ewelme and its surrounding chalk hills. It also offers views westwards over the vast expanse of Benson's RAF airfield with Benson and the Thames beyond. As usual on many of these walks you can also see Wittenham Clumps and Didcot Power Station in the distance. The walk is easy to navigate and mainly on field tracks.

Ewelme's spring-fed pond opposite the village store.

Most of the route is dog friendly but in the village and passing the pigs east of the village, dogs should be on leads.

No public toilets so rely on those in the Ewelme Store or the Shepherd's Hut pub at the west end of the village (not en route).

Park on Parsons Lane, immediately north of the parish churchyard.

The Ewelme Store in Parsons Lane is recommended, run by volunteer villagers as a charity. The Shepherd's Hut does food at the west end of the village.

The Old Rectory east of the parish church has a postcode of OX19 6HP.

Ordnance Survey Explorer 171.

Ewelme grew up where springs emerge within a dry valley to feed a stream that meanders to join the Thames. The pure chalk stream was well known for its cress beds and at the centre of the village is a pretty pond in which you can see several springs bubbling up (the village's name means a spring source). The landscape of the walk is mainly large arable fields with long views from the tracks we followed.

MIDSOMER COMES TO EWELME

Not surprisingly *Midsomer Murders* came to this beautiful village and was seen in 'Small Mercies', 'Beyond the Grave', 'Secrets and Spies', 'The Black Book' and 'The Sword of Guillaume'. Much use was made of Rabbit Hill where various characters talk with the church, almshouses and school in the background. Indeed in 'The Sword of Guillaume' the characters have their backs to the village but are supposed to be looking out to sea!

A BIT OF HISTORICAL BACKGROUND

Ewelme boasts the oldest church school in England; established in 1437, it lies to the south of the contemporary almshouses built around a cloister, both buildings in fifteenth-century brick. To the east is one of Oxfordshire's finest parish churches, also mostly fifteenth century. Almost all this is the direct result of the endowment by the great poet Geoffrey Chaucer's granddaughter, Alice Duchess of Suffolk. It is an interesting example of medieval social mobility as Chaucer was of tradesman stock, his father a London wine merchant. Geoffrey, who rose in royal service, was England's foremost poet until Shakespeare's time and schoolboys of my generation studied his *Canterbury Tales* at school, usually the 'Prologue' and the 'Pardoner's Tale' (rather duller than the racy 'Miller's Tale', we felt). He prospered sufficiently for his son, Thomas, to marry the heiress of Ewelme, Maud Burghersh. Their daughter, Alice, married into the aristocracy, firstly marrying the Earl of Salisbury and then William De La Pole, Earl and later Duke of Suffolk: quite a rise in status within three generations.

What we see today in Ewelme is a direct result of Alice's piety and devotion to good works. The almshouses, named God's House, were founded – along with the school – in 1437, and both were built soon after. The almshouses provided for thirteen almsmen and two priests, one to teach the children of Ewelme in the new school. All of the almshouse inhabitants were to pray constantly for the souls of Alice and her family.

These are remarkable enough survivals and you can freely visit the almshouse's tranquil cloister, but the church is quite exceptional: a church of East Anglian quality transplanted into the Chilterns. The reason for this, of course, is obvious,

Rabbit Hill where various Midsomer Murders' *characters talk, while the church, almshouses and school appear in the background.*

as Alice was Countess and then Duchess of Suffolk. I don't want to catalogue its marvels, just urge you to visit and spend at least a richly rewarding hour inside. The tour de force, I think, is the monument in finest English alabaster to Alice herself, who died in 1475, the upper one sublime and peaceful in rich mourning robes, the lower her cadaver in a traceried cage contemplating for ever paintings of the annunciation that only the effigy's half-closed eyes can see. Clearly this whole monument was the work of the finest and most skilled of royal master masons and sculptors from London. Others regard the towering timber font cover as a remarkably rare survival.

A superb church in stone and flint with brick battlemented parapets, it is architecturally all fifteenth century, except for the lower parts of the west tower which dates from a century earlier and are all that remains of an earlier church. From the west door a covered way links the church to the almshouses and the complex is in some ways best seen from near Rabbit Hill. Also, within the churchyard and south of the church itself is the gravestone of Jerome K. Jerome who was buried here in 1927, the author of two great gentle and warm-spirited comic novels, *Three Men in a Boat* and *Three Men on the Bummel*. How fitting that he should rest in this quiet churchyard in the Chilterns not far from his beloved River Thames.

THE WALK

1. Again lucky with the April weather, after we had visited the outstandingly interesting church and the almshouses, we set off along Parsons Lane in sunshine with cotton wool clouds hanging in the blue sky. We walked east away from the village and the church, passed The Old Rectory, its chequer-brick outbuildings fronting the lane, and bore left at a footpath sign on to the Chiltern Way. We followed a track that soon became a grassy path, hedged initially. We emerged on to open downland, the track broad and grassy, a new hedge on our right with a post and wire fence beyond.

After a while we reached what my uncle used to call a 'Pig's Peacehaven' (he lived in Sussex), a vast array of miniature Nissen huts occupied by pigs and their piglets. We continued ahead past the pigs and, enjoying expansive views, descended to reach the lane out of Ewelme. We bore left along the road, a young, mixed copse on our left and glimpses of Britwell Salome house and its urn-crowned column (see Walk 17).

The Ewelme village store cheeseboard.

2. Reaching a bridleway sign about 100m before the road bore to the right, we turned right on to the bridleway. The track crossed a shallow dry valley, the fields bright with yellow oilseed rape flowers in April, a hedge on our left. The track continued across another dry valley, the hedge now to our right, and uphill to reach a footpath crossways. We continued ahead past a coppice, the track now climbing amid hedgeless fields, descending at length into another dry valley.

3. We bore right at the cross paths by a footpath guide post. We followed the track, the hedge initially on our left, then along both sides. Ascending to a footpath post we passed to the left of it to continue ahead. Reaching a T-junction of tracks we turned right and passed farm buildings, then continued ahead by a footpath sign along a hedged track, named Potters Lane on the map, with views of Didcot Power Station and Wittenham Clumps (Walk 16) in the distance. The track descended from

Ewelme's colourful fields.

Ewelme village store.

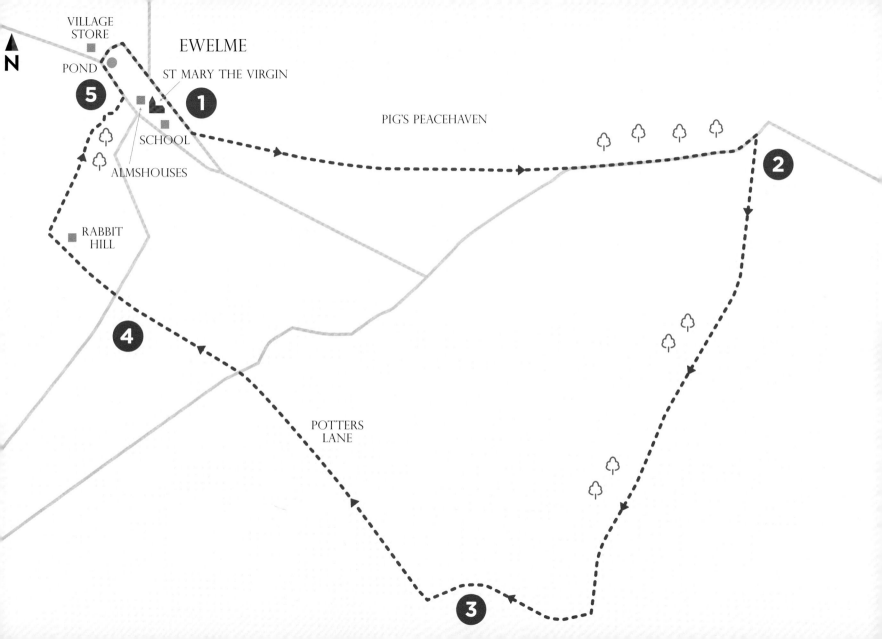

the crest towards Ewelme, still between hedges, and we reached a lane that we crossed to continue ahead on a narrower footpath, old gravel pits to our right. Ignoring a path off to the right we continued ahead to reach and cross another lane.

4. We continued ahead between post and wire fences with views down over RAF Benson, Benson itself and the huge tiled-roofed eighteenth-century brick barns of Fifield Manor. To our right, beyond the pasture of Rabbit Hill, was Ewelme church. Reaching a stile we turned right to continue alongside the post and wire fence, an arable field to our left. The path descended to the corner of the field and we continued ahead within trees and past a stile, then between gardens and on to a gravel drive that led to the village road in Ewelme. We turned left into The Street and walked along this pretty road to the pond, with its attractively landscaped margins. This is one of the spring-fed sources of the Ewelme Stream and its former cress beds.

5. Here we turned right into Parsons Lane and had some welcome food and refreshment in Ewelme Store which has a couple of benches and a table outside as well as a few tables inside. The building was a Wesleyan Methodist chapel built in 1826 and had been converted into a shop years ago. After being closed for a decade the village took it on and it reopened in about 2008. Ever popular with walkers and cyclists as well as villagers, village volunteers (together with a paid staff member) run the shop and cafe. The food was excellent and we continued along the lane past the village pound where stray animals were kept until reclaimed by villagers who would have had to pay a small fine for their carelessness or their sheep or cow's ingenuity in escaping their field. A sign says it was last used in the 1930s. The lane bore right and led us back to the churchyard and the end of the walk.

WALK 18 'COPTERS AND GREENS 4.5 MILES (7.2KM)

Benson and Warborough

INTRODUCTION

This walk is a relatively easy one on the flat valley where the River Thame meets the Thames with a long stretch along the Thames bank while the inland stretch is through the rich and vast arable fields that lie between Benson and Warborough. The route between Benson and Warborough is on farm tracks and there are few navigational problems.

The route combines the flat river-valley fields and meadows with basically flat arable 'champion' country. On this walk you have distant views of hills and only a few gates to negotiate along the Thames.

The route is dog friendly apart from within Benson, Warborough and Shillingford. From Shillingford to Benson you follow the Thames Path National Trail.

Public toilets are in the car park in Benson where the walk starts and in The Six Bells pub in Warborough.

Park in the free public car park in Mill Stream, off the High Street behind the Co-op in Benson.

The Six Bells in Warborough is beautifully situated, does good food and is featured in *Midsomer Murders*, although is closed on Mondays. In Benson the Waterfront Cafe is by the River Thames.

The postcode for houses adjacent to the car park is OX10 6RP.

Ordnance Survey Explorer 171.

Shaded River Thames path.

MIDSOMER COMES TO WARBOROUGH

Clearly the *Midsomer Murders* location team found Warborough more to their taste than Benson, which is too busy when compared with the former's large green that lies off the through road. The Six Bells pub on the green featured in several episodes and changed its name to The Black Swan in 'The Great and the Good', The Quill Inn in 'Sins of Commission' and to The Luck in the World in 'The Second Sight'. Opposite the church, The Aisha Stores, where you can get hot drinks and a sandwich or pie, featured as did several other houses and cottages in the lanes at the west end of the green in such episodes as 'The House in the Woods', 'The Great and the Good', 'Market for Murder', 'Bad Tidings', 'The Night of the Stag' and 'Sins of Commission'. Looking at the village you can see why it was chosen so often.

The grandest house chosen was the manor house on the south side of the green, a tall, stone house with brick dressings and a date stone of 1696, which was used in 'The Sicilian Defence' as Edward Stannington's house.

RAF Benson helicopters fly around Wittenham Clumps.

A BIT OF HISTORICAL BACKGROUND

Benson was the centre of a great Anglo-Saxon estate but remained a large village until the eighteenth century when it acquired a number of coaching inns on the then new turnpike road from London to Oxford via Henley. Part of this route was removed when Benson aerodrome was built, the Benson end being helpfully named Old London Road and the route resuming on Beggarsbush Hill beyond the aerodrome. Benson prospered and four large coaching inns were built in the eighteenth and early nineteenth century: The White Hart and The Castle inns at the west end of the High Street and two others on the High Street, The Old Red Lion and The Crown Inn. All except The Crown Inn are now private houses or apartments. The coaching age only lasted from 1736, when the turnpike opened, until the Great Western Railway branch to Oxford opened in 1844. Thereafter the coach trade withered and in 1873 the road ceased to be a toll road. The village has expanded much since the war, some of it not attractively, which has reduced the architectural quality of stretches of the High Street and other old roads.

Benson's RAF station pre-dates the Second World War but not by much, work started in 1937 and it opened in 1939. It had a key role to play in the war and focused in the later part on aerial reconnaissance. Nowadays it seems populated almost exclusively by helicopter squadrons and the sky around Benson is often dominated by their noise: you can't hear the skylarks when a Chinook is in the air!

Charles Buckeridge mainly rebuilt Benson's St Helen's church in the nineteenth century. He also built the charming Tudor-style brick and flint vicarage at the north end of Church Road (No. 11). The thirteenth-century nave arcades survive and the aisles are basically fourteenth century but Buckeridge restored them with a somewhat heavy hand. The west tower is a Georgian one in Classical style with round arched windows in its ashlar elevations. Work started in 1765 but foundered and had to be completed in 1781 when the belfry stage was added. Fortunately Buckeridge retained this tower: he must have liked it as it is hardly 'correct' Medieval Gothic. The other striking features inside are the blue panels in the roofs, which introduce a somewhat jaunty air.

Cricket on Warborough Green.

THE WALK

1. On a cloudy late April day, we left the car park in Mill Stream, a cul de sac off the High Street, and turned right into High Street, passing the punningly named fish and chip shop, 'The Village Plaice', and turned left just past The Crown Inn into Crown Lane. At a small triangular green we bore to the right and continued ahead, passing a children's playground, then left into Hale Road.

Soon we left the village houses behind and, now on a farm access, continued ahead, passing Hale Farm, an early nineteenth-century house with chequer brick walls and a hipped slate roof. Now on a hedged track we passed the farm buildings. Where the hedges ended we continued ahead to a footpath post.

2. At the footpath post we turned left on to a track between arable fields with views ahead of the Wittenham Clumps (Walk 16). We crossed a footbridge to continue along the track and crossed another stream or drain. The track became

The Six Bells on Warborough Green. It was The Black Swan in 'The Great and the Good', The Quill Inn in 'Sins of Commission' and The Luck in the World in 'The Second Sight'.

a hedged lane and emerged at the east end of The Green in Warborough. Passing the *Midsomer*-featured manor house, the cricket pitch and a slate monolith commemorating the Queen's Diamond Jubilee, we reached The Six Bells for a drink and a snack lunch.

3. This area at the west end of the green was intensively used in *Midsomer Murders* and we spent a happy few minutes 'location spotting' before continuing on our walk. From The Six Bells area we went along the lane to the right of a former chapel and then left at No. 23 on to a footpath that leads into the churchyard.

We were fortunate to meet a local who told us a lot about the history of St Lawrence's church and pointed out the late twelfth-century lead font, some fourteenth-century stained-glass fragments and the Prince of Wales feathers painted on the chancel side of the chancel arch. These are Stuart and the initials 'CP' refer to a Prince Charles, whether the prince who became Charles I or Charles II he did not know.

We left the churchyard via the lychgate and turned left, passing the war memorial. We continued south on a pleasant path running parallel to Thame Road, noting the exposed cruck truss on the side of No. 109 Puddleduck Cottage and the row of whitewashed and attractive modern cottages, Nos 111 to 115 designed by Lionel Brett who later became Lord Esher. We passed St Lawrence's Church of England Primary School and, where the main road bears left, crossed it to continue ahead on a footpath beside a stream and parallel to Warborough Road. We continued ahead to reach the main Oxford to Wallingford road, the A4074.

4. We crossed the main road and were now in Shillingford village, passing the spectacular and ancient wisteria that draped itself along the garden walls and front of No. 6, named, unsurprisingly, 'Wisteria Studio'. In late April the wisteria was at its delicate best.

Soon we reached Shillingford Wharf; now no longer a commercial wharf, it is a pleasant green space on the Thames bank flanked by a thatched boathouse on the right, a splendid weeping willow and another grander stone boathouse and Swan Cottage. On the corner of Swan Cottage are flood markers showing levels reached by spectacular historic floods of the Thames, the highest having been in January 1800 and well above our head height.

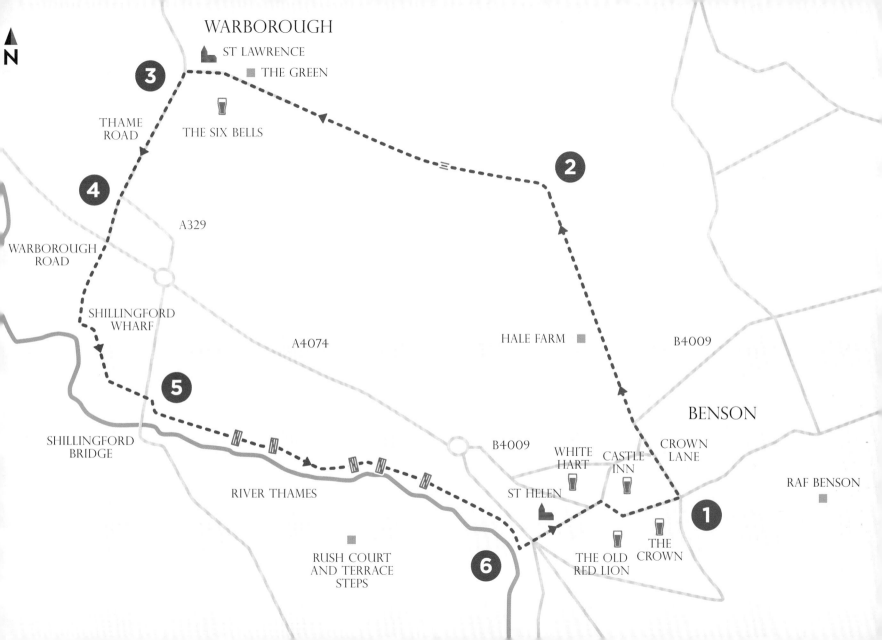

We followed the Thames Path National Trail to the left of these flood markers along a path between garden walls. At a T-junction of paths we bore right to continue between walls and fences and past the gates to Shillingford Court. We passed through a kissing gate to join a lane and continue left along it. Reaching the road we turned right towards Shillingford Bridge.

5. Shillingford Bridge is an elegant three-arched one built in 1827 to replace a ruinous timber one of 1767. Both were toll bridges but this ceased in 1874 when it was handed over to the joint care of the counties of Oxfordshire and Berkshire (the south half was in Berkshire until 1973) and became toll-free.

On the Oxfordshire side the approach causeway is about 300ft long and we descended left at a footpath sign, just before reaching the bridge proper, to walk alongside the approach causeway's fine stonework to reach the river bank, still on the Thames Path National Trail.

The path along the riverbank passes gravel pits, new and old, with views back to the bridge, usually partly obscured by riverbank vegetation. Through a hand gate we continued, looking across to the former Berkshire bank where we saw the grand, stone riverside terraces and landing steps of Rush Court. This is a Victorian mansion, much extended and now a care home, but the house itself is not really seen from the Oxfordshire bank. We passed through three further hand gates and over two footbridges. Through another gate the path continues through a marina with big launches moored to the bank and log cabins inland.

Houses and cottages on Warborough Green have been seen in such episodes as 'The House in the Woods', 'The Great and the Good', 'Market for Murder', 'Bad Tidings', 'The Night of the Stag and Sins of Commission'.

6. At the Waterside Cafe we went left to the main road, the A4074, and crossed it, turning right to pass a bus stop. We turned left into Church Road and shortly into St Helen's churchyard where fortunately the church was open.

From here we continued northwards to the war memorial cross beyond which is evidence of the village's eighteenth-century coaching importance: the long white-painted building to the left was The White Hart of about 1820. Facing us was the long front of the former Castle Inn, the main range in Georgian stone with brick window surrounds and to the left a bow-fronted addition in grey brick with red window dressings. This splendidly closes the vista and the original elaborate wrought-iron inn sign survives. In the High Street we had at the start of the walk seen The Crown Inn, another of the coaching inns but the only one still in use as a pub. At Castle House we turned right and walked along the High Street, passing The Court House on the right; this building is Georgian with arch-headed box sashes, it was The Old Red Lion and the fourth coaching inn, and acquired its name because Charles I is reputed to have held court here during his flight to Oxford during the English Civil War (the core of the building is seventeenth century). Past this we reached the Co-op and the end of our walk although, sadly, not in the most distinguished part of Benson architecturally.

The colourful interior of Benson church.

Benson church's bright red door.

Warborough cricket pavilion seen in 'Dead Man's 11'.

Wisteria House.

CAUSTON, OR IS IT? 4.25 MILES (6.8KM)

Wallingford

INTRODUCTION

We chose this walk because Wallingford is singularly rich in historic architecture and, indeed, history. The route, besides hoping to lay out the Berkshire town's history before you, also takes in two deserted villages on the east or Oxfordshire bank: Newnham Murren and Mongewell, whose churches are something of a contrast.

 Much of the route is dog friendly but in the town dogs should be on leads and likewise in the fields on the Oxfordshire side if cows are grazing.

 Public toilets at the Riverside Car Park and in Wallingford.

 Park in the Riverside pay and display car park at the east end of Wallingford Bridge (on the Crowmarsh Gifford side of the river).

 There is plenty of choice in Wallingford from pubs to cafes and St Mary-le-More church near the Town Hall serves hot drinks and cakes on many mornings.

 The postcode for Riverside Park where the walk starts is OX10 8EB.

 Ordnance Survey Explorer 170.

Since 1974 Wallingford has been within Oxfordshire. The walk is basically on level ground along each side of the river and there are no real navigational problems.

In the town the route is mainly on roads and lanes but with paths in the parks.

MIDSOMER COMES TO WALLINGFORD

Wallingford was used as 'Causton' in quite a few episodes and we see the Market Place, various streets (including St Mary's Street) and the long medieval (and later) bridge across the River Thames. The 1856 Corn Exchange in the Market Place became Causton Theatre in such episodes as 'Stranglers Wood', 'Death of a Stranger', 'Death of a Hollow Man' and 'Death's Shadow'. South of the market a shop with a light blue shopfront named 'Down to Earth' became the 'Browse Awhile Gift Shop' in 'Small Mercies' and a shop near the Corn Exchange became a jewellers' shop in 'Blue Herrings'. The large stuccoed riverside house, unoriginally named 'Riverside', which can be seen from the Oxfordshire bank as well as in Thames Street, featured in quite a few episodes including 'Blue Herrings', 'Dead Man's 11' and 'Death's Shadow'.

A BIT OF HISTORICAL BACKGROUND

Wallingford as a town dates back to the reign of Alfred the Great in the late ninth century and was one of his new towns or *burhs*. Enclosed by earthen ramparts on three sides, an amazing amount of this survives and you can walk much of it, either on or beside the rampart or the deep outer ditch below. The ramparts were topped with timber palisades and the only loss was after William the Conqueror passed through the town and the castle was built across the east part of the ramparts and occupying the north-east quarter of the town.

The river provided the east boundary and in the Middle Ages the town thrived and you can still see old malthouses, barns and warehouses, mostly near the river. At one time it had a dozen churches within its ramparts, although these dwindled to four by the seventeenth century. Three survive today, one with a fair amount of Anglo-Saxon masonry and, of course, much of the street plan also dates back to the ninth century as the only major alteration was the widening of one street to form the long marketplace, presumably around 1100, if not before.

The river and its trade were key to the town's prosperity until Abingdon supplanted the town in the fifteenth century when its new bridge crossed the Thames there and became the county town. Wallingford was besieged during the English Civil War and the castle was 'slighted' or destroyed at Oliver Cromwell's orders in 1642.

Wallingford's relatively narrow river bridge includes a long causewayed approach with a mix of thirteenth, fourteenth and sixteenth-century pointed arches and even a twelfth-century round-arched one. The main spans date from the eighteenth and early nineteenth century and until widened in the 1770s it must have been jolly narrow.

Wallingford's ancient defensive ditch.

The River Thames at Wallingford.

This introduction can do little justice to this most interesting and historic town with its wealth of historic buildings from all stages in its history, culminating, we suppose, in the Waitrose building opened in 2005.

THE WALK

1. We started the walk, on a drizzly May morning, from the Riverside car park where there is also an open-air swimming pool and a campsite. We passed under one of the medieval arches of the Wallingford Bridge causeway, going left alongside it before bearing half right to merge with a footpath and passed through a kissing gate. We continued ahead, alongside a hedgerow on our right. To our right, beyond the river, a long stuccoed house, Riverside, can be seen which was used in *Midsomer Murders*. Through another kissing gate we continued

ahead towards farm buildings and passed to their left via another kissing gate. We left the farmyard through a field gate and bore right on a lane, then ahead on a track to the left of the Newnham Farm sign.

2. A little way along, past the farmhouse, we turned right into a yew tunnel through the hedge to a gate into St Mary's churchyard. This, the farm and its cottage are all that remain of Newnham Murren village, whose parish was a long narrow strip of fields that ran from the riverbank 6 miles east into the Chilterns. The village disappeared probably in the sixteenth century and the parish is now within Crowmarsh Gifford, as is Mongewell, the next deserted village on our route.

The church is entirely hidden from the river and a tranquil gem. Mainly Norman, if over-restored, inside it has a brass memorial on one wall with a musket ball hole from the siege of Wallingford in 1646 during the English Civil War.

Out of the church we rejoined the hedged track and passed under the Wallingford by pass to join the Ridgeway National Trail. Just before a terrace of painted flat-roofed houses we turned right to follow the signs to St John's church.

We passed through the grounds of the former Carmel College, which closed in 1997, its buildings looking unloved. It utilised Mongewell House and added large numbers of highly modernistic buildings within an eighteenth-century landscaped park. We reached the gate into the churchyard and from here we could see some of the modern buildings across a narrow eighteenth-century lake.

3. The church itself, like Newnham Murren, is basically in Norman flint but a most odd one. The nave roof has gone and at the west end is a curious hexagonal Gothic tower and an apse, also added in 1791. Inside the restored chancel are two mighty Georgian memorials, one to John Sanders of about 1731 with him reclining on his elbow holding a book, the other of 1692 with two portrait busts. Quite an unusual interior, we felt, but wonderfully situated near the river.

We retraced our steps through the grounds and then headed left, back beneath the bypass again, before turning immediately left to cross the river over its bridge. Over the river we turned right and descended a ramped path to a gate. Through this we bore half left through buttercup-rich pasture and merged with the

The large stuccoed riverside house, unoriginally named 'Riverside' is featured in 'Blue Herrings', 'Dead Man's 11', and 'Death's Shadow'.

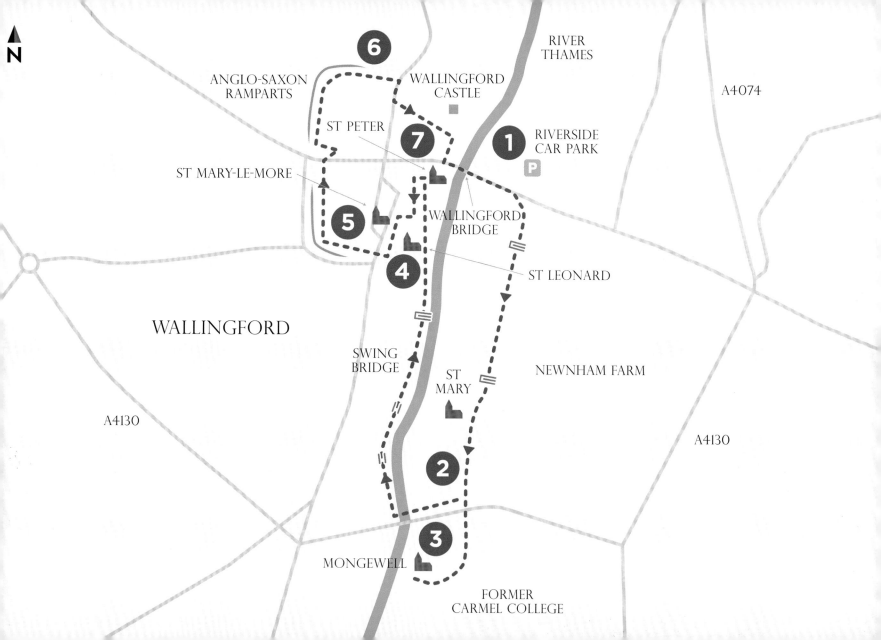

N

RIVER
THAMES

A4074

ANGLO-SAXON
RAMPARTS

WALLINGFORD
CASTLE

ST PETER

1 RIVERSIDE
CAR PARK

7

ST MARY-LE-MORE

WALLINGFORD
BRIDGE

5

ST LEONARD

4

WALLINGFORD

SWING
BRIDGE

ST
MARY

NEWNHAM FARM

A4130

A4130

2

3

MONGEWELL

FORMER
CARMEL COLLEGE

Thames Path along the riverbank. We followed the riverbank, initially in pasture and, beyond a hand gate and footbridge, through a series of narrow fields ending at the riverbank. We crossed another footbridge, across Bradford's Brook, which marks Wallingford's parish boundary, then passed a former Thames Conservancy building of 1913 built above an arched flooding basement with various markers of historic flood levels. Shortly we passed the rather grandiose 2007 buildings of the Oxford University Boat Club via a swing bridge.

Reaching the end of a lane, Lower Wharf, with an old malthouse and a sixteenth-century jettied house on the left, we turned right on a path through a brick house and over a footbridge.

Wallingford meadow

4. We followed the path that emerged by St Leonard's church, which shows its Anglo-Saxon origins in the herringbone stonework high upon its nave wall: apart from the town ramparts this is probably the town's only Anglo-Saxon remains that survive above ground. Continuing northwards along the Thames Path route in Thames Street, we passed the porch to the stucco-fronted Riverside house that was used in *Midsomer Murders* and where, a plaque by the door informed us, the Victorian landscape and domestic life painter George Dunlop Leslie lived

St Mary's church, Newnham Murren.

Plaque on Riverside, Thames Street.

from 1884 to 1907. His sister Mary, also a painter, lived in Cromwell Lodge next door. We passed the gates and high garden walls to Castle Priory and turned left into St Peters Street. These lanes are basically those of the Anglo-Saxon *burh* and we turned left at the T-junction, soon turning right into Mousey Lane which leads to the marketplace, passing the side wall of the Corn Exchange Theatre which, of course, featured in *Midsomer*.

5. The marketplace was carved out of the Anglo-Saxon town by 1155 when the town got its charter from Henry II. The Town Hall of 1672 is a fine one and dominates the marketplace with the church of St Mary-le-More behind it. We continued past the church, on St Mary's Street, noting the shop 'Down to Earth', which had been used in *Midsomer Murders*. Continuing ahead and beyond St Leonard's Square we turned right into Mill Lane, just beyond The Partridge pub. We passed on our left a timber-framed former barn or warehouse and continued ahead, now on the Anglo-Saxon ramparts and past Croft Terrace, cottages built for the workers at the old Wilder's iron foundry in Goldsmith's Lane

(now converted to dwellings). To our left was the Anglo-Saxon ditch below the ramparts, which we followed where they turned north. At a path junction we bore half right across the park, Kine Croft, to the main road, heading for the flint-built Wallingford Museum, its seventeenth-century flint facade concealing an earlier medieval building.

6. We turned right, crossed the entrance to Goldsmith's Lane and crossed the road left to enter Bullcroft near the sign to the Citizens Advice Bureau. This park was the site of Wallingford Priory, founded in 1097. We went left past the Citizens Advice Bureau along a path beside the rear garden boundaries of the High Street towards a stone column. This was a gas lamp standard of the 1830s, moved here from the marketplace as a parkland ornament in 1921. Here we turned right to follow the ramparts, descending steps at the end to a footbridge. Over this we bore right along a footpath beside the ditch but now outside the Anglo-Saxon defences.

Wallingford parish church.

Thames flood-level mark.

Reaching the road via steps we turned right, the castle earthworks on our left, leaving the road at the footpath sign to the right of No. 24, a rendered and slate-roofed cottage. The path wound between walls, screening views of the castle earthworks, unfortunately, but in fact passing through its bailey or walled courtyard below the keep mound. Bearing right on to a tarmac lane we descended to the road and turned right briefly, then left to visit Sir Robert Taylor's St Peter's church just in Thames Street.

7. St Peter's church is Georgian and has a wonderfully evocative pierced spire in Gothic style. Sir William Blackman, who died in 1780, is buried in the churchyard and the church attracts numerous American visitors as his 'Commentaries on the Laws of England' – besides being influential in England – undergirded and framed the American Declaration of Independence and the new country's constitution. We retraced our steps and walked back across the river bridge, descending steps back into Riverside and the car park.

STEAM RAILWAYS

WALK 20 PANNIERS AND CEMENT 5 MILES (8KM)

Chinnor and Princes Risborough Railway

INTRODUCTION

Obviously the focus of this walk is the Chinnor and Princes Risborough Railway with its terminus at Chinnor Station. It's less of a mouthful to abbreviate its name to CPPR for the rest of the walk details. The walk crosses the line three times, goes alongside it and visits Wainhill Crossing with its level crossing and station halt. After the small town of Chinnor the route heads out into the fields to the hamlet of Henton before heading back to the railway. The route follows roads in Chinnor itself and in Henton but is otherwise on field paths and tracks.

The route combines delightful open countryside and views south to the well-wooded Wain Hill and The Cop on the Chiltern escarpment. The only livestock when we walked it were ponies in paddocks around Wainhill Crossing.

MIDSOMER COMES TO CHINNOR, WAINHILL CROSSING AND HENTON

The centrepiece of this walk, Chinnor Station, appeared in 'Death in a Chocolate Box', but with the usual change of name. The station became Holm Lane Junction while further up the preserved railway line Wainhill Crossing halt also appeared, dramatically changed in the same episode with automatic gates temporarily replacing the current painted-timber level-crossing gates.

Chinnor's High Street also featured in 'The Made to Measure Murders' episode, Dillamore's shop being used as Woodley and Woodley, the tailors. Nearby No. 19 was used as Trevor Minchin's House, also in that episode.

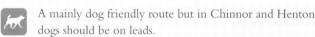 A mainly dog friendly route but in Chinnor and Henton dogs should be on leads.

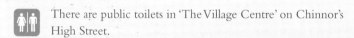 There are public toilets in 'The Village Centre' on Chinnor's High Street.

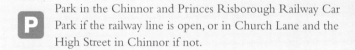 Park in the Chinnor and Princes Risborough Railway Car Park if the railway line is open, or in Church Lane and the High Street in Chinnor if not.

 The Peacock in Henton does superb food and there are several pubs in Chinnor.

SAT NAV CPPR car park, OX39 4PR.

Ordnance Survey Explorer 171, 181.

At the southern end of the long, straggling hamlet of Henton, Allnutts Farm, once known as Bachelor's Farm Cottages, appeared in 'A Rare Bird' and was used as Ford's house.

A BIT OF HISTORICAL BACKGROUND

Chinnor Station is the terminus of the Chinnor and Princes Risborough Railway, a preserved railway line that took over the northern section of the Watlington branch when the line to Chinnor Cement Works closed in 1990, giving it about 3.5 miles (5.7km) of track. The stretch between Chinnor and Watlington had long closed and the track had been lifted, its last goods train (of empty mineral wagons) had run in 1960. The lost sections can be seen on Walks 8 and 9.

Chinnor Station is a superb replica built by the CPPR in the late 1990s and reconstructs the original one that was sadly demolished in the 1970s.

The line had originally opened in 1872 as the Watlington and Princes Risborough Railway but was taken over by the Great Western Railway in 1883. Except on special occasions, the line currently does not get quite as far as Princes Risborough Station but the CPPR live in hope of a more permanent link.

It was first built as a light railway, which meant its track work was designed for lighter locomotives and rolling stock. Indeed, when the Great Western Railway took over in 1883 they found that the track had been poorly constructed and laid on bare chalk without ballast. It unsurprisingly had to be completely re-laid to a much higher standard. Moreover the old railway had only two locomotives and a few carriages and wagons.

Allnutts Farm appeared in 'A Rare Bird'.

An unusual gravestone, Chinnor.

Health and safety at Wainhill level crossing.

Chinnor Station appeared in 'Death in a Chocolate Box', but with a change of name to Holm Lane Junction.

The CPPR started its services in 1994 and now uses a mixture of Great Western pannier tank engines and diesels to run its trains and mostly operates at weekends. It is always worth checking their website for timetable details. Generally speaking, steam runs on Sundays and diesels on Saturdays. There is a cafe in an old Cambrian Railway coach body built in 1895 on the platform next to the station building.

THE WALK

1. From the CPPR car park we crossed the main road and went left across the bridge over the railway. We soon bore right at a 'No Entry' sign on to Church Lane, which curves to the right. At a junction we turned right and went through the tile-roofed lychgate to visit St Andrew's church, Chinnor, which is often open during the day. It is quite a large and interesting church with a thirteenth-century nave, aisles and west tower and a fourteenth-century chancel. Besides some good medieval stained glass, the timber chancel screen is particularly interesting, being reputedly one of the earliest surviving in an English parish church and probably dating from the 1320s. From the church we continued towards the shops.

2. Next we headed north along the High Street. As we passed the Congregational church graveyard, we saw a gravestone with an anchor projecting from it to one Thomas Spencer Jackson, buried in 1888, presumably an old salt. At the T-junction we turned right by The Red Lion on to the main road, Lower Icknield Way, then shortly left into Holland Close.

We continued ahead in Holland Close and soon left Chinnor's suburbs behind, emerging into a countryside of large arable fields. The track reached a modern barn where we continued ahead across an arable field and then alongside a hedge. Crossing a footbridge and passing through a kissing gate we continued ahead, still alongside a hedge to another kissing gate. Here we turned right on to a track.

3. Reaching a T-junction we turned right on to a tarmac lane, which we followed to Henton, ridge and furrow in the last fields before we reached the hamlet. At the T-junction we turned left to walk through Henton, a mix of older houses, some timber-framed, others Georgian and later brick, and modern infill housing.

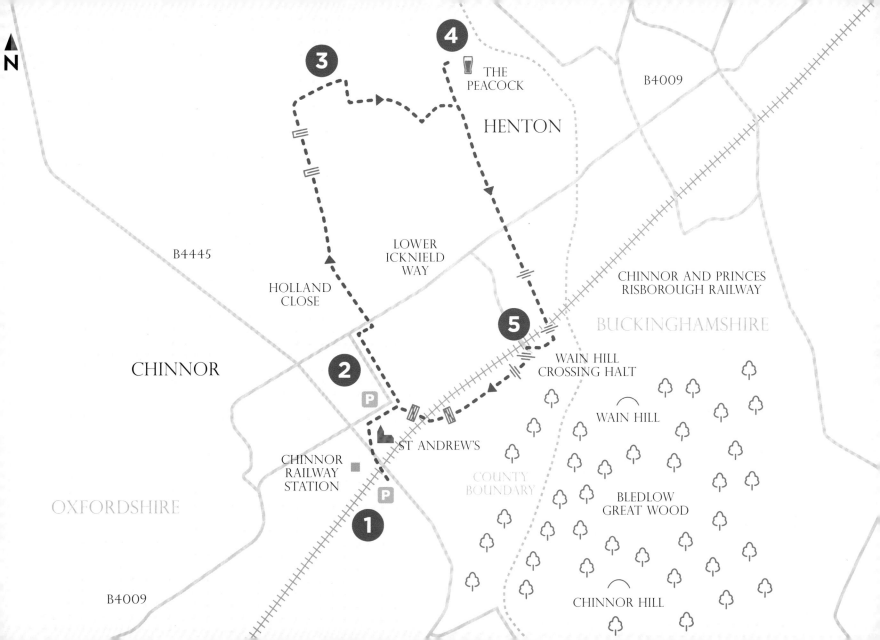

4. At the end of the village we bore right to The Peacock Country Inn where, as usual, Martin Roberts made us most welcome and we lunched there. The Peacock is a partly seventeenth-century timber-framed house, now the bar area. We retraced our steps through the whole village, the footpath parallel and to the west proving impossible to negotiate. We passed the timber-framed Allnutts Farm that featured in 'A Rare Bird' and soon left the village, continuing to the main road, the B4009.

At the main road we turned right for a few yards, then crossed diagonally right to a footpath sign. We walked southwards alongside the hedge, 'Wainhill' on the footpath sign. Ahead is the railway line and we crossed it via a stile on each side of its single track. We crossed the paddocks to leave over a stile in the corner of the field. Bearing right we headed for another stile, continuing ahead between a house and barn to another stile.

5. Over the stile we turned right again on to a lane that led to Wainhill Crossing. This is a level crossing on the CPPR railway and also a modest station halt, signed 'Wainhill Crossing'. It was something of a latecomer to the Watlington branch and only opened in 1925, some half a century after the line first opened. The former crossing-keeper's cottage is now a private house but the station has been lovingly restored by the CPPR. You may wonder how busy a crossing-keeper on this sleepy branch line would have been, but virtually every level crossing had someone to perform this role, apart from single farm accesses where the farmer operated the gates.

We retraced our steps and at Thatched Cottage's name sign rejoined the footpath, turning right on to a track. Jinking past gardens the path then follows a track parallel to the railway line, eventually reaching a hedged lane that has descended from the Ridgeway and the Chilterns. Here we curved right, re-crossing the railway line again via hand gates. Disappointingly these are modern steel gates, not historical replicas as at Wainhill Crossing.

We followed the lane as it curved left, now back in Chinnor. Turning left back into Church Lane we bore left past the parish church, still on Church Lane, and back to the CPPR car park.

WALK 21 METRO COUNTRY 4.5 MILES (7.2KM)

Buckinghamshire Railway Centre, Quainton

INTRODUCTION

The focus of this walk is the Buckinghamshire Railway Centre (BRC) at Quainton Road Station, a fascinating place to visit with live steam trains on certain days. Starting in the delightful village of Quainton, we criss-cross existing and former railway lines, including the famous Brill Tramway, and pass through classic Midland landscape corrugated with the ridge and furrow of pre-Enclosure Act common field strip farming. The route follows some lanes in Quainton and near the BRC but has at least two thirds of the route on field paths and tracks.

The route mostly combines delightful Midland hedged fields with views of the sheep-cropped Quainton Hills to the north and Waddesdon Manor (Walk 5) away to the south on its tree-girt hill.

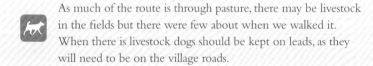 As much of the route is through pasture, there may be livestock in the fields but there were few about when we walked it. When there is livestock dogs should be kept on leads, as they will need to be on the village roads.

There are no public toilets so rely on the George and Dragon or the BRC.

Park around the village green in the centre of Quainton.

The George and Dragon on the green in Quainton is friendly and welcoming and the food is good. There is also a cafe at the BRC.

SAT NAV The George and Dragon in Quainton has the postcode HP22 4AR.

Ordnance Survey Explorer 181, 192.

The railway runs through the middle of the house. The route of HS2.

MIDSOMER COMES TO QUAINTON ROAD STATION

The Buckinghamshire Railway Centre is another railway venue that has featured in a couple of episodes: 'Down Among the Dead Men' and 'Things That Go Bump in the Night'. In the latter it became Fletcher's Cross where a village fete was held. Its role in 'Down Among the Dead Men', though, was more fleeting with Barnaby and Jones standing on the road bridge looking down into the station.

Quainton village, with its fine green sloping up towards the windmill, appears not to have featured in any episodes.

A BIT OF HISTORICAL BACKGROUND

This being a preserved railway-themed walk, this background section concentrates on the railway heritage. The first Quainton Road station was opened on the Aylesbury to Buckingham line, which took a westward course for the convenience of the 3rd Duke of Buckingham who lived then at Wotton Underwood. The station opened in 1868 and the duke then built a horse-drawn tramway from Quainton Road to his estates at Wotton, soon extending to Brill in 1872. It was converted to steam and became part of the Metropolitan Railway but was closed in 1935. The Metropolitan also took over the Aylesbury and Buckingham line in 1892, terminating at Verney Junction where a large hotel was built to encourage tourism and rail traffic but remained distinctly non-metropolitan, ending in deeply rural Buckinghamshire.

The third line here was the Great Central, which opened in 1899, the child of the Manchester, Sheffield and Lincolnshire Railway, which changed its name and headed for London with the last main line built into the capital. Two lines have disappeared except for trackbeds, the Brill Tramway (1935) and the line to Verney Junction (lifted in 1953). The old Great Central survives as a freight-only line as far as Calvert from 1966.

The Quainton Railway Society was formed in 1969, just three years later, and has gone from strength to strength. The station has been restored and Oxford's Rewley Road terminus, which had opened in 1851 and was in many ways similar to Paxton's Crystal Palace, has been re-erected at Quainton. An exciting project supervised by local architect Lance Adlam gives the centre a long train-shed

Metropolitan Railway level crossing keeper's house.

building for static train displays, a museum, bookshop and a cafe. There are steam and diesel locomotives here and you can visit the centre's website for details of when they are running. You can go round the centre even when no trains are running and we have visited on numerous occasions, often with grandchildren when there is a Thomas the Tank Engine day or a Santa Special at Christmas time.

THE WALK

1. We set off from Quainton's village green on a crisp, sunny February day with clear blue skies and occasional clouds, heading west from the fifteenth-century stone village cross into Upper Street. The house behind the cross has the date '1723' on a stone panel with the carved coat of arms of the local Dormer family, many of whose monuments are in the parish church (Point 6), while beyond it is the tall tower windmill built in 1830, currently without its sails.

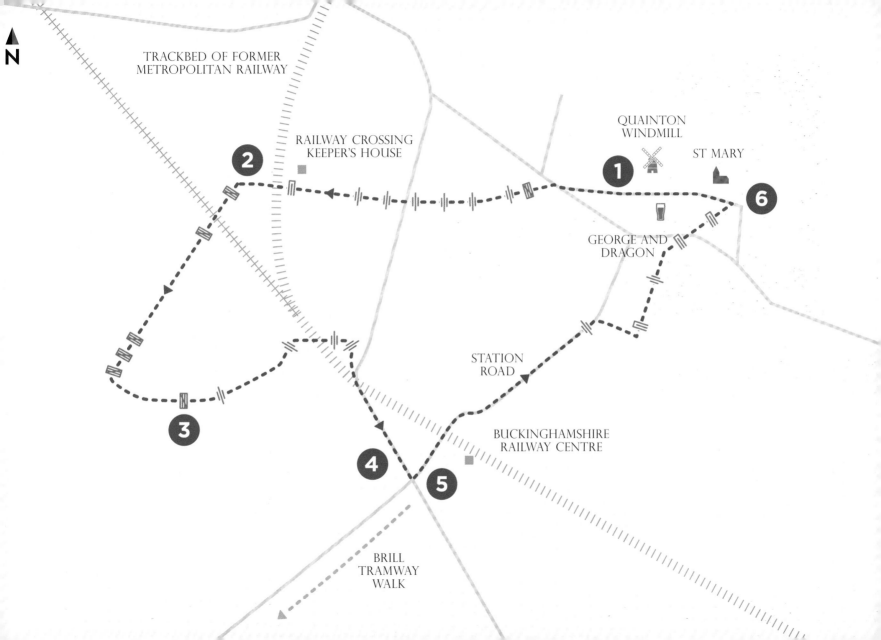

N

TRACKBED OF FORMER
METROPOLITAN RAILWAY

RAILWAY CROSSING
KEEPER'S HOUSE

2

QUAINTON
WINDMILL

ST MARY

1

6

GEORGE AND
DRAGON

3

STATION
ROAD

BUCKINGHAMSHIRE
RAILWAY CENTRE

4

5

BRILL
TRAMWAY
WALK

161.5 miles to Manchester by train but not since the 1950s.

Where Upper Street merges with the main road through the village, we crossed it and at Klee Close we went left to a hand gate on to a footpath to continue ahead across pasture. Across a double stile and footbridge we continued ahead alongside a hedge, in ridge and furrow pasture with a view of Waddesdon Manor away to the left. Over another double stile and footbridge we took the right-hand path and continued ahead to a hedge gap with electricity pylons beyond. Over yet another double stile we headed to another stile on to a lane.

We crossed the lane, over a stile and traversed a small pasture to a double stile and footbridge at the left of a tree belt, then another stile to continue ahead along a metalled track, mercifully free of stiles for a while.

2. Reaching Railway Cottage we crossed the trackbed of the old Aylesbury and Buckingham Railway, later the Metropolitan Railway, the cottage a crossing-keeper's. Beside it we saw a rusting iron Metropolitan fence post with an ornate finial while the field gateposts are also railway ones. We continued ahead through the kissing gate alongside a hedge, arable to our left. At a tree the path bore left across the field to a gate in the hedge and we crossed the railway line via

The view from Quainton to Brill on the hill in the distance.

Quainton village in the sun and the rain.

field gates. This was the old Great Central Railway line, opened in 1899, which connected London to the north. Currently it only carries very long waste trains as far as Calvert, about 5 miles north-west of Quainton Road Station. Much of this is the spoil coming at present from the Crossrail work in London.

We continued ahead alongside some post and wire fences, Brill Hill away to our right (Walk 1) and Waddesdon Manor to our left (Walk 5). We crossed a farm lane via two field gates and then bore left, aiming to the left of farm buildings ahead across excellent ridge and furrow pasture. Leaving the field through a field gate we turned left on to a farm track, then very soon right over a stile where we headed half left across arable to reach a stile in a post and wire fence.

3. Instead of climbing the stile we turned left alongside the fence to rejoin the farm track. Over it we crossed a stile and a footbridge to head half right to a kissing gate to cross another farm lane and then through another kissing gate in more pasture. We crossed the railway track again via a stile, then up steps to another stile. Before heading across the field to the right of a cattle barn we looked along the trackbed of an old railway that diverges from the line we had just crossed. This is the line of the old Aylesbury and Buckingham Railway whose tracks were lifted in 1953. We noticed that its trackbed was at a higher level than the existing Calvert line we had just crossed. We passed over a footbridge with a stile at each end to reach a road.

Here we turned right and crossed the railway again looking down on railway archaeology with a surviving line and the start of the curve of the old trackbed of the Aylesbury and Buckingham diverging away. We saw a plaque with '161' on the north side of the bridge which is a Great Central affectation as they measured

distance from Manchester's Piccadilly Station rather than the normal mileages from London termini. We continued along the lane to a crossroads.

4. Here we turned left, passing a footpath sign for the Brill Tramway Walk which heads south-west from Quainton Road, and crossed the railway bridge, looking right to the Buckinghamshire Railway Centre and its Quainton Road Station, as did Barnaby and Jones.

5. Across the railway bridge we continued along Station Road, the houses on its right-hand side clearly filling much of the gap between the railway station and Quainton village nearly a mile away. Where the road bears left we went right at a footpath sign just before a memorial bench to a Norman Price. We crossed a stile and continued ahead along a track, passed a field gate and then left through a kissing gate to continue ahead towards Quainton, walking parallel to a hedge and a stream. We crossed a stile and a footbridge to continue ahead through the edge of a small housing estate, initially on a gravel path, then a grassy one.

Reaching the village road we went briefly right, then crossed to a kissing gate beside Tuesday Cottage. We continued alongside a hedge on our left, through another kissing gate and then between a hedge and a post and rail fence, a good view of the many gabled windows and tall chimneys of the almshouses near the parish church on our left, and crossed a footbridge. Through another kissing gate we bore left to the gate into Quainton's churchyard.

6. The church has some superb and very grand seventeenth and eighteenth-century monuments, mostly to the Dormer and the Winwood families. The most human one is at the west end of the south aisle, curiously cramped, with Richard Winwood lying in his armour and his wife up on her elbow looking tenderly down on him. The church is worth visiting for the monuments alone.

From the churchyard we walked west along Church Street, passing on our left the Winwood Almshouses with the Winwood coat of arms and the date 1687 in each Dutch-gabled porch. This was the same Richard Winwood whose effigy we had just seen in the church (he died in 1689). There are good houses along this road, an old village water pump and also the village store. Back at the green we finished the walk still in bright sunshine, and went to the George and Dragon for lunch.

Fellow walkers about to stroll to the Wittenham Clumps.